If you have to ask the question 'why?' you wouldn't understand the answer.

This book reconciles the madness of the ultra distance with the magic of the moment to give an insight into why more and more people are running trail ultramarathons for fun.

Nobody Tells It Like This Guy!

Mixing the intensely personal with the clinically professional, Andy Mouncey tells his story using three different and sometimes completely contrasting perspectives: As a fierce competitor, as an experienced coach, and as self-employed husband and father just trying to find his way in the world.

The brutal honesty, penetrating insight and tension-busting humour will suck you in and keep you engrossed even beyond the finish line.

If you do endurance sports, you will get this. If you don't do endurance sports, you will really get this – and you will never have to ask the question 'why?' again.

It's Not About The Distance

This is a transformational personal journey that was revealed only when Andy paused to look back - and it's also an utterly compelling tale of some long races in great places where he ran as fast as he could for as long as he could. Sometimes it worked, and sometimes...

About The Author

Andy Mouncey was born in Leeds, West Yorkshire, UK. After 17 years in triathlon in 2003 he set fastest stage times for the Enduroman Arch To Arc Challenge: a 300 mile solo triathlon linking London and Paris via an English Channel swim. He then hung up his goggles and turned to ultra-marathon running. He is a professional speaker, trainer and coach who has appeared on radio and TV.

He is married and lives with his family in the north of England.

www.bigandscaryrunning.com

andy@doingbigandscary.com

07799 063 115

What They Said

'*Magic, Madness and Ultramarathon Running*' takes you on many journeys along trails, over mountains and down dales but on one very special journey - into the psyche of Andy Mouncey; record holder and experienced ultrarunner. His narrative style and internal conversation put you right there at that moment. You feel the wind, the rain, the frustration and the elation in the same way that watching climbing movies make your palms sweat.

Andy provides great insights into how he prepares for and executes key races - marshalling not only all his own experience and motivation but the power and support of friends and family too - with this book you see how running very long distances alone is actually a team sport. You also see the comedy, some of it tragi-comedy, that accompanies our endeavours; at one and the same time massively important and totally irrelevant.

If you dare to dream and love the outdoors I suggest you fill your pockets with gels, grab a waterbottle and sit down for a long read.

MARK HARTELL
LAKE DISTRICT 24 HOUR RECORD HOLDER AND 11 TIMES FELLSMAN CHAMPION

It's a frank insight into the exciting and often hilarious world of an elite endurance athlete; it will inspire weekend warriors and well worn ultra runners alike.

It'll appeal to anyone who's ever put one foot in front of the other in the pursuit of adventure.

GAYNOR PRIOR
LAKELAND 100 WINNER 2011

The massive highs and the painful lows, the view around every corner, the next checkpoint, the finish line, the support and supporters, team mates and family, the company of other runners etc.: you have said it all, each moment a fantastic memory. Your book certainly made me smile, feel the pain, laugh and dream a bit more. Nothing will happen unless we dream it first and my dreams are starting to scare me.

SHARON MCDONALD

I have had the good fortune of knowing Andy since I took him on as coach way back in 2006 for my first Ultra. He has been an inspiration and good friend over the years and it is a joy to read his race stories. Having read the book it has enforced my desire to do more stupidly long races so I can either blame him or give him credit for it (depending on how bad or good I am feeling at the time!).

JO KILKENNY

This book is an intriguing read as Andy travels along his emotional journey of discovery and learns what it is to become a successful ultra trail runner. Andy transforms from focusing on the physical: the pain, the suffering, and over time evolves into the 'aware' runner, able to not only write about what should be happening / what he should be focused on, but eventually able to actually experience it, to feel it, to live it.

As with the journey of life, the messages are not always obvious, not always easy to see. But if you read this book with an open and receptive mind, and are able to feel beyond the race descriptions, then what is really important within ultra trail running (and possibly life) will hopefully become that little bit clearer!

I encourage you to implement endurance qualities and read the entire book without taking lengthy breaks. An uninterrupted passage alongside Andy as he travels through his transformational journey will enhance your journey and assist you in learning from Andy's experiences.

STUART MILLS,
7 TIME BEACHY HEAD MARATHON CHAMPION, LAKELAND 100 WINNER 2010

The chronological structure of the book is a great insight into the years of dedication needed to cope with the pressure of competition, and the learning that only comes with experience. The 'you'll have good days/months/years, and bad days/months/years, accept it, be patient, be in the moment' theme is beautifully expanded in the book.

GEOFF COX

Magic, Madness and Ultramarathon Running

Andy Mouncey

Published by Filament Publishing Ltd

16, Croydon Road,
Waddon, Croydon,
Surrey
CR0 4PA

Telephone +44 (0) 20 8688 2598

email: info@filamentpublishing.com
www.filamentpublishing.com

Printed by Berforts Group

ISBN 978-1-908691-26-2

Typesetting and Cover Design Charlotte Mouncey www.bookstyle.co.uk

Cover Photos Phil Coates www.philcoates.tv www.alpine-oasis.com

Credit for other photos in the book with thanks to:

Geoff Cox

North Face

Phil Coates

Rory Coleman

Steve Bailey

Stuart Mills

Tim Jury

Dedication

To all to those people who make it possible for us to play:

Race organisers

Marshals

Checkpoint staff

Event crew

In particular to Lakeland 100 Race Directors Marc Laithwaite, Terry Gilpin and all their fantastic folks

Special Thanks

Sharon Macdonald

Jill Eccleston

Jez Bragg

www.jezbragg.blogspot.co.uk

Mark Hartell

www.markhartell.blogspot.co.uk

Gaynor Prior

www.purepersonaltraining.co.uk

Jo Kilkenny

www.jokilkenny.com

Geoff Cox

www.rsvpdesign.co.uk

Annie Dawson

www.alpine-oasis.com

Dr Artic

www.philcoates.tv

Peter Addison-Child

Stuart Mills

www.ultrastu.blogspot.co.uk

Their comments and reactions on the final draft reassured me that I was on the right track and helped me improve the final version immeasurably.

Yes, the little things really are the big things.

Cover design, layout and formatting is courtesy of my extremely talented and gorgeous wife Charlotte who can be reached at www.bookstyle.co.uk

Staggeringly sharp editing by our lovely neighbour Margaret Ellis.

The fantastic cover photos are by kind permission of Phil Coates
www.philcoates.tv www.alpine-oasis.com

For the numerous pictures in the book additional thanks to:

Geoff Cox

North Face

Phil Coates

Rory Coleman

Steve Bailey

Stuart Mills

Tim Jury

Preface

They think it's madness, what some of us do for fun - but as someone once said to me when explaining why she was habitually evasive about her weekend ultrarunning activities to her work colleagues on a Monday morning, 'If they have to ask the question why, they wouldn't understand the answer anyway.'

That's right: They wouldn't - and couldn't - understand the magic.

I started running in my teens at school, then was absorbed by triathlon for 17 years, and then in 2003 I got my introduction to ultra running - except that this baptism came as just the first stage of a 300 mile London to Paris triathlon challenge in which swimming the English Channel was the wet bit in the middle.

My Enduroman Arch To Arc Challenge was a life-affirming event. Some stuff did indeed change for me as a consequence - the main one as far as this book is concerned is that I stopped swimming - otherwise you'd be reading something along the lines of Magic, Madness & Ultra Distance Racing. Since early 2004 I have not turned a stroke in anger - just couldn't get my head around swimming pools after the open sea - and so turned my attention to journeys on two feet.

What follows on these pages are the ultrarunning race experiences which shaped me as a runner and refined me as a husband, father, eldest son, brother, and just a curious bloke trying to figure his way in the world. Or if you want the simple version it's also just a collection of some long races in great places where I tried hard and went as fast as I could for as long as I could. Sometimes that worked out and sometimes…

I've also tried to put the races themselves in some sort of context by going back through my old diaries and pulling out what else was happening on Planet Mouncey at that time. A vastly illuminating exercise it was as well - and a reminder that not much that happens to us does so in isolation.

This all means that what you have here is an intensely personal account spanning nearly 10 years. It's also completely my take on the races and what was happening around me at the time. Fellow competitors I was locked in battle with may well have a different perspective. No slight is intended whatsoever. I like to construct scenarios in my mind that help me when racing - these scenarios just have to be plausible enough to feel real and I've tried to be honest about recounting that stuff here.

You'll also notice some changes along the way - not least of which is that my writing style has evolved somewhat. That's because all these race accounts were written at the time, which makes the early stuff ten years old.

I hope you enjoy it for what it is.

For me, it's all still is very much a work in progress.

Andy Mouncey 2012

Foreword

I can still clearly remember the moment I first met Andy. It was late summer 2004, in a field, in the heart of the Worcestershire countryside. It was the eve of the Marathon of Britain, a gruelling multi-stage race across the heart of England, an adventure like many of those you will read about in this book which bonds a small group of like-minded runners together like no other. There is nothing like a tough, weeklong, ultra distance race to forge lifelong friendships. And so our paths had crossed.

For both of us, that was our first venture into the slightly obscure and some would say 'underground' world of ultra running. Since then I have regularly seen Andy at the big races around the UK and beyond, and it's fair to say that if you see his name on the start list, it's not going to be an easy race.

When you meet Andy, the thing that will strike you most is the energy which comes with him. Always. It's infectious; you can't help but feel lifted and buoyed by his approach, attitude and mannerisms. You certainly won't be disappointed in the energy found in this book either – it shines through in every sentence!

In reading this book you will soon realise that Andy's ultra running career is just the icing on the outside of his career; his many preceding years spent in other areas of endurance sport make his performances, consistency and general drive, actually quite hard to comprehend. Andy competes, finishes and often stands on the steps of the podium, time after time.....

Ultra running is of course about being fit and durable, but more than that it is about your approach and attitude. The race tales and experiences Andy has pulled together in this book provide an inspirational insight into how he has gone about achieving all that he has in the sport, becoming one of the most consistent performers around. There is a lot to learn. I hope you enjoy his stories like I did.

Jez Bragg 2012

Winner Ultra Tour Mont Blanc 2010

Jez enjoying himself at Western States 100
Photo: Facchino Photography

Contents

In The Beginning Was Triathlon...

It had been a swim-bike-run lifestyle since 1986. I'd done most things I could reasonably aspire to: The iconic nearly-ironman distance race in Nice, France twice, GB Age Group representation at European Duathlon and World Olympic distance triathlon, ironman half a dozen times. The bright star of Hawaii was missing, but I'd missed my chance with that one.

Those first ten years were almost total immersion. Training was regularly done in a group of like-minded fanatics and we'd just go out and try to kill each other. Leg shaving, Oakley sunglasses, hideous fluro colours, weird handlebars – even bike helmets, for god's sake! Everything was geared around the next workout or the race at the weekend. We were bomb-proof, tanned, looked great in lycra and I loved it.

I loved thoses shades! Giving it some at Portsmouth 1990

Training groups came and went - jobs, homes and priorities changed and life moved on. As the new millennium came and went I began to drift more and more and look for other challenges: Which brings us to 2002...

2002

Significant for four reasons:

1. Charlotte and I get married in May - I was so happy I cried!
2. I get to attend the Commonwealth Games in Manchester as part of the triathlon event organising team where 75,000 people rock up to watch the best in the old empire swim-bike-run
3. New wife has a big messy mountain bike crash right in front of new husband in the middle of nowhere
4. At the end of August I go beyond Ironman for the first time and get my introduction to the world of ultra distance racing at the three day Enduroman Chesil Beach challenge

The start of the year finds me working with a triathlon coach for only the second time in my career. Bill Black makes sure I do my homework as I get ready for the regional duathlon champs in April. Looking back at the sessions and there's some serious work going on here – around 8-10 hours a week - and I am clearly on intimate terms with my turbo trainer.

My diary notes frequent tiredness and sleeping problems in the first four months or so due to a combination of business and training stress – reading it back now it's obvious I'm just too damn wired most of the time. I'm two years into working for myself and flying around all over the place from our base near Leicester saying 'yes' to any remotely income generating opportunity.

I'm Conditioning Coach to a bunch of world class swimmers and loving it – but I've yet to learn how to screw the lid down tight to prevent 24 hour leakage...

A diary entry June 24 reads: 'Saw an article on Enduroman Chesil. Oh dear, I think I'm interested...'

I arrive at Chesil Aug 29th full of doubts and focusing on what has been missing from the previous six weeks of preparation. In the event, what has remained proves more than enough and I get to meet Mr Enduroman Eddie Ette who will change my world over the following year.

The year rounds off with my first K2 canoe race over 60km round the canals of Birmingham in October. One capsize and a torn shoulder ligament later and it's off on the winter club cross country carousel.

Enduroman Chesil 2002: Taking The Plunge

August 30th - September 1st Chesil Beach, Portland, Dorset

Day 1: Swim 8 miles

Day 2: Cycle 150 miles

Day 3: Run 27 miles

Diary extract post-Chesil:

How nervous was I before this?! My physical prep had been pretty much zero due to a combination of work priorities, feeling crap, Common-wealth Games, and Charlotte's accident. I didn't really know what to expect – and the swim scared the hell out of me. I figured 16 years in the sport was worth something. My general level of conditioning was good. I believed I could do it – I just didn't 'know.'

The goals in order were:

- *Finish the swim intact*
- *Complete the bike and run without killing myself*

Feeling small and scared at Chesil

What a three days! Taught me much about my general condition and mental approach. The whole thing is such an achievement given the last six weeks or so – made all the more special because this was a new race.

I was smiling stupidly for the first time in many weeks – such a tonic! Bring on double ironman!

"How you feeling?" shouts Paul my accompanying canoeist. I pause while making a grab for the bow of the boat. I'm about 200 yards off Chesil Beach in 70 feet of water which is about 16 degrees centigrade - pretty warm, they said. My situation has remained more or less unchanged for the last three hours or so during which time I've been enjoying the freedom of swimming in the open sea: it's just that I'm now at the interesting part. I'm starting to feel sea-sick and am trying to stop myself retching on mouthfuls of seawater. My eye sockets hurt from the goggles, I can't face any more rice pudding and I'm slightly pissed off that Randy the dolphin hasn't appeared yet.

I try to estimate the distance still left to swim. This is a mistake because Chesil Beach from this angle looks like a ramp of pebbles which extends as far as the eye can see. This is because it is a ramp of pebbles which extends as far as I can see: I know this because I'd looked on the map and had decided not to use the shoreline to measure how far I'd swum because it all looks the same along this bit of coast as well as a heck of a long way on the map!

The plan was to get my head down and swim for 45 minutes then stop and feed. Coffee, rice pudding and an energy drink all courtesy of Pauls' Meals On er...A Keel (?) service. Do this for three times then drop down to 30 minute efforts definitely NOT looking for the finish! How can I spot the finish from the water surface in a hefty swell from any kind of distance when I don't even know what the bloody thing looks like anyway?!

Things however, are definitely getting interesting: I've made good progress over the first half but am now swimming against the current, the swell is up, it's clouded over and I'm cooling down despite the full body wet suit which is now starting to chafe against the crook of my arms and the base of my lats. And I really am feeling very sick. This is just not funny anymore and it's definitely not like this in the brochures. Oh well, this is still the furthest I've ever covered, (my previous being two and a half miles) and I always knew the 2nd half of this little 10 mile paddle would make or break me - if I let it.

So I steel my mind and simply say, "I'm OK, I'm just feeling a bit sick - just give me a minute will you?"

A change of goggles - these ones are a slightly different fit - a few mouthfuls of coffee and half an energy bar are consumed while I scan the surrounding ocean. I can see two canoes which mean two other swimmers: one about level with me nearer the shore and one not too far ahead. I try to remember how I and the other 13 swimmers settled down after the first half mile or so...that must be either the leader or the second place swimmer ahead of me then. I bin the thought quickly: today is not about that. Just finish in one piece, but please Lord, make it soon!

Paul is stowing kit in his boat - he must have a numb arse and probably needs a serious piss by now - and looks at me: " Not far now, you've nearly cracked it." I grimace. "Give me a shout in 20, will you?" A few strokes on my back to ease the kinks out then I flip over and sight on Paul slightly ahead and off my right shoulder as he has been for most of the swim. I get my head right down to ease my neck for a few strokes then move back into my pattern: a few strokes of bilateral breathing, then left then to the right then sight on Paul and back down again. I'm finding that the bilateral breathing smooths the stroke out and stops me bobbing around as much. This is good as it minimises the seasickness. OK, let's see if we can close on that wetsuit ahead...

Fish-like swimming before the collapse at Chesil

There's a canoe to my left and it's not Paul. I move slowly past the other swimmer. He or she - I can't tell - is breast stroking so must feel worse than I do. Paul must be chuffed to bits as it's someone else to talk to after hours leading some rubber-clad idiot through the sea on his own. I silently wish him well as I've got enough on my hands just maintaining my own swim discipline.

Shit, this really hurts! Wouldn't it be great to see that damn dolphin now? Swimming with the big fish off the English coast - how cool would that be! (We'd been told at the briefing to watch out for the dear chap who has been spotted around the coast. Don't worry if he gets close, they said: he just likes neoprene rather a lot. Let's hope the name isn't too literal then…).

I stop dead. It's as though someone has flicked a switch. I want to scream, cry - do anything except bloody swim! Am I even making progress anymore? And while my head falls apart a lone swimmer passes to my right. I barely register it. I crane my eyes along the shoreline. Where the **** is the finish?!? Paul catches my mood: "You're going for the tent - see it?" What bloody tent? All I can see is pebbles! "How far?" I shout in desperation. "400 yards!" 400 yards. Oh **** it, get your head down and just go: you're a coach, you're supposed to be able to do this head stuff - walk the walk, remember?

Don't look up, don't even think it - just keep swimming, keep swimming - you'll get there.

So I re-pass my swimming nemesis for the last time and crawl shorewards right on Paul's stern and then I can see it - the bloody tent at last! C'mon, just get there and then you can stop. three strokes and breathe left, three strokes and breathe right, three strokes…Thank Christ! I'm washed unceremoniously ashore…and then just as unceremoniously out again. Jeezus! I just want to stop now please! Second time in and this time I am grabbed and unceremoniously hauled out. I just register it is Eddy Ette (Race Organiser and Man Whose Idea All This Was) who is on haulage and rehabilitation duty and I know he has been anxiously awaiting the return of his charges. I know it's really important to tell him I'm OK, but the urge to sit down heavily and slump beats me. C'mon, get it together! I slowly raise my eyes and look back over the sea and start to smile. Ed catches my eye and then we're both laughing as the tension vanishes and the achievement starts to sink in: Game on!

For the record

Seven swimmers set off for the long seventeen miles or so and forteen of us for the 'short' effort. Most people hadn't done anything to compare with this - ever - and though only four out of twenty-one did not finish, it was a day of massive achievement all round - not least for all those involved in the safety cover. Many, many thanks to you all!

After four and three quarter hours in the water, my second day consisted of ten and a half hours in the saddle. This included just about every hill in Dorset - and it's hilly! - and a chance to put our feet up during a ferry crossing three and three-quarter hours later. At the end of the third day I had probably seen most of Dorset - some bits from many different angles. Yeah, it was just a little bit special for everyone involved: we felt the fear...and did it anyway.

2003

The Big One. Fellracing fun till May then it's all about getting ready for 300 miles of run-swim-bike between London and Paris in September with a terrifying English Channel swim as *only* the wet bit in the middle. Eddie Ette's Enduroman Arch To Arc Challenge has been tickling me over the winter. The tickle becomes and itch and then...

I'm still wrestling with the highs and lows of self-employment and doing periodic stress at shocking cashflow and blank pages in the work diary. That's focusing on stuff you can't control, then... Charlotte and I commit to A2A in March and then shortly after I promptly lose my biggest income source. I get serious about the prep from May – which pretty much revolves around getting ready to swim the English Channel *after* running nearly 90 miles and before riding 180.

You can read the full story in London To Paris The Hard Way – for now, I'll give you some of the highlights from my diary noted after September:

- Ten days to stop passing out and sleeping like a corpse for 10-12 hours a night
- Three weeks to stop feeling sore
- Two months to even vaguely feel like pushing it again

For Charlotte and I, it was a life-enhancing experience in ways we never imagined, so here's the run stage to give you a sense of just some of that.

roman Arch to Arc Challenge 2003: First Run 87 Miles To The Beach

Wednesday September 16th 2003

Morning - and Charlotte and I are at home doing a piece to camera on the eve of my A2A Challenge: 300 miles of running, swimming and cycling between London and Paris with an English Channel swim as the wet bit in the middle.

"It's all less than 10 hours away now: the start has been moved forward and we're enjoying a last quiet moment. We were due to go on Thursday, but there has been much excitement in the house since this morning when we got the phone call from Portland: 'We're gonna go now - get your ass to London!'

So I'm here trying to do calm - really I'm a bit butterflyie - and Charly's doing very excited.

How excited are you, Charly?"

She leans in close and her face shines: 'I'm very excited!'

The phone's been going mad and that includes BBC TV: 'Hello, we're the BBC and we're interested.' 10 hours to go and NOW they're interested!?!"

Turn to face excited wife. "Why am I doing all the talking, Charly?"

"Cos you're so good at it, Andy!"

Fair one. Back to camera...

"So we've got a little jog at night through London. I figure it'll be quiet but they're trying to tell me something about a 24-7 capital city - probably having to run the gauntlet with kicking out time from the clubs: impromptu speed session anyone? Tomorrow we see the sea, which means it's swim-time. I plan to rest - how long? We'll see, but it'll be a start in the early hours. 12, 13, 14 - 16 hours, I don't know: I've done the training and I'm just confident I can do it. Touch the French side then get back in the boat for the ride to Calais - how weird is that?!? Then there is just a little bike ride to finish with the last 30 miles into the heaving, seething metropolis of Paris. Navigation will probably be the only thing on the minds of the crew - but I can ride like a Parisian if I have to."

There's three key points in my mind on this jaunt for me:

1. Finish the swim,
2. Ride up Avenue des Champs-Élysées
3. Talk to rooms full of people about the whole thing afterwards.

And I'll take 'em all - especially the first one.

The rest of the day passes in a whirl of preparations. I had planned to sleep but it just never happens, and by 9.30pm we are en route to the start.

"We're coming into London, Andy" Charlotte shakes me gently out of the short sleep I've managed to grab in the back of the motorhome and I peer out of the back window. Yep - definitely London and definitely very real! We share a nervous smile and I move to sit next to her knowing that this will probably be the last quiet moment together for the next few days. I watch the increasingly familiar sights roll past as Charly helps her brother Tim who is driving to find our way to Marble Arch where we are due to link up with The Two Eddies' - Clarke, our main driver, mechanic, navigator and all round top bloke, and Ette - whose World Record I'm out to take.

The final member of our crew is sitting opposite me having finished a full day in his osteopathic clinic barely two hours before. I met John Williams some three years ago when he was lecturing on a sports massage course I was attending when I was getting ready to start my own business. We clicked, found out we lived and worked pretty close together and stayed in touch. For the last two years or so John has fixed every single one of my coaching clients I have referred to him. As far as I'm concerned his professional competence is 24 carat gold - though that fact that we share the same hairstyle really clinches it. He has become a firm friend to both Charlotte and me, and I know my legs will be in great hands on the first stage.

John catches my eye: "How you feeling?" I nod slowly and let a smile grow. "I'm good, I'm alright." He smiles and looks away as Charlotte squeezes my hand: not long now...

And then we're there. Tim does a circuit of Marble Arch as the rest of the guys strain to spot signs of The Two Eddies. Sure enough the unmistakable outline of a small white van is parked unashamedly centre stage, and while Tim only baulks slightly at the prospect of getting 30 feet of motorhome through the Arch itself, pride dictates he manages it on the third circuit - well, we all figure we've got a great excuse to be here - and as the time edges towards midnight we roll to a stop.

Greetings and introductions are exchanged. The last time I saw Eddie Ette was some two weeks ago at my last training swim off Portland. The handshake is as firm as ever but the eyes say 'showtime!' He looks straight at me: "How you feeling?" I give it straight back: "I'm good - so how do you want to play this, then?"

I let him make the running as I figure this part is probably more nerve-racking for him as it is for me. It's as much a first for him as it is for me and we've both invested in the other to get at least this far. There's friendship and mutual respect in abundance and we've both seen enough of the other over the summer to know that we will both give everything we have to pull this off...we just don't know if this will be enough. I'm reminded of a phrase from my old triathlon club days: 'When the flag drops, the bullshit stops.' Guess we're gonna find out, then.

Once we're away the crew will work out and settle into a routine much of which will be dictated by ME: right now it's a little like arriving early at a party - no one wants to be the first to dance! The guys default down to their primary roles: Tim will be doing all the filming and photos and has a whole host of new toys to play with. He travelled down to us from his home in Lancashire on Monday and promptly took over our living room table as a home for cameras, bits of cameras and instruction manuals for cameras! This will very definitely be a 'learn by doing' experience, so he heads off to set up with John being co-opted for floodlight duty. Charly and Eddie Clarke review the route and make final preparations to the vehicles while Ed casts round for someone to grab as a witness signature which we need periodically to validate my progress for the Guinness Book of Records. Something along the lines of 'yes, I did see some idiot running past me at such-and-such a time at such-and-such a place trailed by a dubious looking bloke on a mountain bike, and no, it's none of your business what I was doing out so late on a weekday when most normal people are safely tucked up in bed.' For my part, I have complete faith in Ed's unique ability to co-opt anyone he cares to and relieve them of their signature as we make our way to Dover.

Time to get ready. I keep it slow and methodical and retreat to MY primary role. Running around like an idiot will not help me or the crew: I know the value of role models and KNOW that the guys will take a lead from me throughout this trip. If I'm cool, odds are they will be too, so I go about my final preparation without flapping.

It hits me how warm it is - heat of the city and all that - but I'm sure the temperature will drop as we head out of the city and chase the dawn. I elect to start in shorts and short sleeves. Vaseline goes onto the insides of both thighs and between both sets of toes, soles of my feet and heels and Achilles tendons. I've discovered single skin anklet socks over the summer and now don't use anything else: they're lightweight, breathable, quick-drying and do not ruck up. A small rub could quickly escalate and cause me serious problems. I've been careful during training to look after my feet and keep good foot hygiene - nails are kept short and smooth and callouses are filed down and smoothed off. I will change socks and re-vaseline at every stop with a shoe change at 50 miles. If it happens it happens - but I'm confident my feet will stay intact. A fluoro vest and flashing red light clipped into my waistband completes the ensemble.

Midnight, Marble Arch, London
On the threshold of something big with Eddie Ette

Outside once again and it strikes me how small Marble Arch is - I'm sure the French one is HUGE compared to this! Charly and Eddie C are talking route - the crew will split into two for this first section through London and we will rendezvous with Tim and John in the motorhome at the first stop at 20 miles. The boys are still playing with the technology so Ed and I gravitate towards each other. Conversation is about getting out of London in one piece: stay cool, relax and enjoy the sights - take it real steady and don't get freaked if we lose the route. It's big ole London Village, everyone is a tad nervous, it's all very new and everyone wants to get it right: mistakes are bound to happen. For some reason were talking in low tones - a way to keep the tension at bay, I guess.

It's getting close: Ed hands me some cards from the Weymouth chapter of my support crew and Charly and I go in front of camera to open them: Tom, Kate, Wendy, Lynne and Ed have all sent best wishes in their own inimitable style. Kate has enclosed some photos of her own Channel swim on the most glorious of days and some of Ed getting ready for his. By the expression the camera has captured on his face, I'm relieved to see that he clearly does nerves after all!

Ed's message is all vintage Ette: 'You took the biggest step when you made the decision - now just finish the job.'

I remember his letter of a week ago:

Dear Andy

We have spent many hours together since our first discussions about attempting the Enduroman Arch to Arc. I knew after our first meeting your character was right for the task.

You have come a long way in a very few months and in my opinion are well ready for the attempt. You know the Enduroman Team and I will be doing everything in our power to help you achieve my record. You are being guided all the way by the same Enduroman Team that helped me achieve my 2001 World Record.

As your day approaches many local people have asked me why would I spend so much of my time to help you beat my record. The reasons for this we have discussed many times. It is my opinion that your attempt will highlight the Enduroman Arch to Arc challenge to the world. It is my intention to stage this challenge for any athlete from any part of the world that has the ability to succeed...

The task you have ahead of you is massive. I know because I have been there. You are more than capable and now only require three things: True Enduroman Grit. Fine Weather and Good Luck.

Eddie Ette

Time to go: Eddie has his witnesses, the boys are ready with the toys and there's no more reasons anyone can think of to hang around. A kiss from Charly, a final check of the direction, touch the Arch with my hand and Ed starts the clock at 12.38am. The handshake is firm and the eyes say it all: let's finish this thing!

I take my first tentative steps across the courtyard and down the steps into the subway then angling up to road level trying very hard not to think of the magnitude of what lies ahead. We will pretty much follow the line of the A20 all the way to the coast but I suspect this first bit will be interesting. Ed catches me up on the mountain bike as I take in the sights and sounds of the capital city in the early hours. I'm rubber-necking big-style as I pass The Ritz: there's still plenty of people about and I would hardly say the traffic is light! I'm keeping it smooth and loping along grinning stupidly. I barely get a second glance from those I pass - clearly very little suprises the worldly wise folks down here.

The first hiccup comes after barely the first mile or so: we lose the van with Eddie C and Charly. The motorhome has gone ahead to the first stop at 20 miles but the plan has been for the van to stay as close as it can to us through the city. Easier said than done through these streets with various one-way options even at this time of night. Ed is understandably concerned but I'm cool. I can survive for 90 minutes if I have to, though I'd prefer 60! All we have to do is stay heading for the A20 and the van can backtrack for us: just do my thing and enjoy the sights. I let Ed know I'm not flapping and hope the reassurance helps his nerves. He's already settling into a routine of racing ahead to accost potential witnesses then catching back up to shout directions. I wonder how different this feels for him now...

A few miles later we have our happy re-union with the van and every-one tries hard not to be obvious about the sighs of relief. I've begun to get a little concerned as the time has ticked by and so have been busy being a tourist by way of distraction. At 1.20am I change from shirt to vest - it really is warm! - have a slurp from a carbohydrate drink and continue to pass the time talking bollocks with the boys. The first of the urban fox sightings happens and I wonder idly how many I'll even-tually see.

Feed two comes a 1.50am with a drink and some food. I know I have to keep these brief but the final balance between movement and rest will be a delicate one. I've resolved not to put a watch on these stops but not to hang about either: get the re-charge I need then get on with it. Charly is finding her way into a routine of doze in van, wave to running bloke periodically out of the back window, and prep the feeds ready for running bloke's arrival. We have rehearsed as much as we feel we need to in the days leading up to departure, but we also know that we'll figure much of it out quickly as we go along. She's one switched-on cookie - one of the reasons I married her really... The key to this learn-by-doing in these early miles is that I must be cool, communicate clearly and preferably in advance what I want and when, so the guys around me get the confidence from a working routine quickly. So keep the effort comfortable, say your pleases and thank yous and remember that everyone wants the same damn thing here! So I concentrate on giving out the positive vibes so that we all settle in as quickly as possible. Happy athlete equals happy crew - pretty simple formula really.

4 minutes later I'm on my way walking away from the feed and gradually breaking into a jog.

From Ed's log: *2.30am Sipping carbo drink. Not drinking much. Pace remains strong. I would be drinking more.*

At 3.50am we stop for the first big feed and massage at around 20 miles - the first big marker. The pace has been very comfortable and I'm pleased with progress. This is John's first real test - so just how well can he massage while being asleep on his feet? It's pitch black, we're parked up by a roundabout on the A20 and I'm covered in my warm gear lying on the couch while John does his thing, Charly says 'hi' and does the food bit, and the rest of the boys voice their displeasure that I'm getting all the tea rations at the moment. I remember that Ed needs at least a cup each hour to function so realise that this must be real trauma for him. Tim briefly appears from the inside of the motorhome looking like death, but the lack of tea also means that there is one more good reason not to be awake. We are now very definitely out of London, the urban fox count is at six and all is well with the world.

20 minutes later I'm back on my feet walking away from the crew to sounds of good-natured abuse: something about they thought I was supposed to be running this?

4.30am. Into the quiet unlit lanes now and the van is behind me with lights full beam to light the way. It's been getting steadily hillier and as I'm trying to keep the effort even I choose to walk up the steep climb of Brands Hatch Hill. We really are chasing the dawn now and I'm at the high point of the run which gives me a breath-taking vantage point of the starlit clear sky and the panorama of much of the southeast below me. The fox count is up to eight and I know we will shortly be beginning the long descent into Maidstone. I wonder how my quads will find that...

From Ed's log: *4.55am. Slight pause and walked, started to run more or less straightaway. We drove alongside and asked if OK. He looked but did not speak. First time he has not spoken. Still running well.*

5.15am and the fox count tops out at 9! I pass Ed coming out of a garage into which he has crawled to get a signature. He looks like death and I take great delight in telling him so. The reply casts aspersions on my parentage so I figure I'm the only one enjoying the graveyard shift. Daylight is almost on us and it looks like it will be a good day.

6.15am and I've stopped about a mile short of the motorhome which is parked up at the second massage stop and big feed. That last section felt longer than the planned 15 miles and I've really been looking forward to the stop for the last couple of miles or so. So I've stopped and am in 'let-the- mountain-come-to-Mohammed-mode!'

From Ed's log: 6.15am. *Stopped for a feed drinking carbo. Got in the back of the van and laid flat with legs raised. Talking to Charlotte. He is OK but just decided ' I have now stopped - let's get the van with the massage here!' phoned van to return.*

7am Just under 6.5 hours gone and about 35 miles covered. Started to walk on no problems. Charlotte will cycle with him for a while.

I'm on the couch while John goes to work. The boys are pissed because Charlotte is being fiercely protective about the tea supply: I'm drinking it and they're not. It'd wouldn't be so bad except they've been tortured by the smell of baking bread from the local Sainsburys for the last few minutes while waiting for me to arrive. Tim comes over and does puppy-dog eyes at my mug of tea: I pretend not to notice.

"So, how you feeling - any problems?"

'Just my quads," I reply. While I've tried to control the long descent down from the high point over the last few miles, the old tell-tale signs are there. If there's a weakness it's my quads which go first and always the left side. Everything else is fine. I've been trying to keep it smooth, but the cumulative effect on this gig is a real killer, y'know?!

John looks up from his ministrations: "Are you on the same camber all the time?" I remember a story I heard over the summer about a Forces guy who yomped from Dover to London all on the same side of the road - and gave himself hip problems for months afterwards.

"No, I'm trying to stay level - in the middle of the road where I can. I've been getting away with that through the night - different kettle of fish now though. Right through the training it's been OK, then right at the end - the last couple of weeks I started to feel it in that left side." I shrug and eye John. "Part of the reason you're here, matie!"

Ed wanders over and steals one of my Jaffa cake treats: "Full moon, half moon - total eclipse!" That TV advert has much to answer for...as Ed wordlessly examines some of John's kit.

It strikes me how different this must seem to Ed - it's world's apart from how he worked his own attempts. All this massage and ministrations - what are you, some kinda blouse? Just get on with it! I also know he respects that I want to do this thing how I want to do it. So we just grin at each other knowing exactly what the other is thinking.

It reminds me of the early days in Portland and the messages both verbal and nonverbal: "You want to do this thing? Just swim! Don't think about it, don't piss about and ask questions, don't worry about where you are and how far to go. Your job is to swim - we'll tell you when to feed and when to stop. You need a couple of sixes, an eight and a 10 hour swim and we ain't got much time - and you wont get there by ****ing about. Yes, it's going to be cold, yes, it's going to be hard: it was the hardest ****ing thing I've ever done. I came to hate that bloody quayside where Tom's boat was - but that's the Channel for you. You want this thing? Just get on with it!"

Ed's just a more a Do-er while I'm more a Thinker - though I've had to work hard at combining the two especially since working for myself. An interesting collision of worlds though...

John continues his work as I remark that I'm very glad he's got his human bag with him as opposed to his canine one. You see, John was at our wedding in 2002 when he got into conversation with Sue my mother-in-law who was administering to her greyhound dog at the time. In a previous life John used to race these things, so common ground was quickly established. For some reason the conversation got round to dental hygiene: "Oh, don't worry," pipes up John, "I've got my bag with me, so I can sort her out now if you want." !!!?!!? What the HECK are you doing with your dog maintenance kit at our wedding?!? Still, John got huge points as far as Sue was concerned, as became forever referred to in that part of the family as The Dog Dentist - oh, the trappings of fame!

I spot Tim still doing bleary really well. "I saw the dawn even if you didn't.

"Yeah, but I've got my long term survival at heart," come the deadpan reply. He's still smarting over the refusal of Sainsburys to open their bakery at five am.

I do a piece to camera.

"7 o'clock and where are we? Just coming into Maidstone." John joins in around a particularly impressive calf stretch assist. "Everyone should try this, don't you think, Andy?"

"Absolutely! It'd save the planet - and everything else..." I continue with the narrative: "When we went to collect the motorhome we were the youngest, fittest and slimmest people there. The average age of the combat soldier was 50 plus, the average size was 18 - feet across. We're welcome back when we're old and fat - hey, we'll fit right in then!"

I finish with a slightly more serious bit: "If I have a chink in my musculoskeletal armour it's my quads. Jarring is a problem - I'm OK if I keep it moving and stay smooth. We'll just manage it for this next section. The Goal is 50. If I do that I've cracked it even if I have to crawl the rest."

8am and getting through Maidstone during the morning rush has been a bitch. It'd taken me the longest yet to get running again from the stop: walk - trot-walk-trot - run for a while till the legs get the message again. Charlotte has been with me on the mountain-bike as she has had to link with the van ahead as we weave through the town. It's a relief to get through but traffic remains very heavy - such a contrast to the quiet I've been used to so far. Still, not much I can do about it and chatting with Charly about silly things helps keep the brain busy.

We're onto long stretches of open main road heavy with traffic as we make our way to the 50 mile stop. The temperature is climbing steadily and I have a healthy sweat on. This is THE key benchmark in my mind - it's all down hill after this though it really is unknown territory. I've planned a couple of smaller 10 mile chunks to get to 70 miles but I really have no idea how I'll find it. Guess I'll be finding out pretty soon…

50 miles is reached in a shade over eight hours. This is a longer than normal stop with a big massage, feed wipe down and full kit change and plenty of talking bollocks. Everyone is smiling and chatting - pleased that we're making good progress and I'm still in good condition. The goal throughout the Challenge is to maximise the physical, mental, emotional and nutritional benefit of the stops - so I am able to look at the next section as a whole new start as opposed to a continuation. It's a bit like a rugby team having a wash and changing into new kit at half time. My powers of recovery have always been good as far back as I remember - all I'm doing now is taking it to another level so I am better able to look at this thing as many small steps as opposed to one 290 mile journey.

I'm back on my feet 45 minutes later and am able to break into a run after a short progressively faster walk. We've decided to break this next 10 miles at five miles - or about 50 minutes at my current pace - and sure enough 55 miles is reached 50 minutes later. It's a quick stop but I can tell Ed is concerned that I'm not drinking enough. The temperature is continuing to climb as 11 am approaches.

Now it's getting real interesting. I find that it is easier to break into a run while going uphill than on the flats or definitely any downhills. My legs are getting progressively stiffer and my quads are more and more solid. Knee lift is limited and I definitely won't win the style prize anymore. 'Just keep moving - keep running.' I remember the line from Lance Armstrong's book: as he goes through his chemotherapy. 'Get up - move! If you can still move you're OK.' I'm not looking into the distance anymore - with the peak of my hat pulled right down over my eyes my vision has narrowed to the 2-3 metres in front of me. Occasionally I'll check to spot where the van is, but that function's been allocated to a distant part of the brain I'm not all that bothered about. Keep the rhythm, keep moving, keep RUNNING - just get to 60 and you'll be OK.

I force myself to break the tunnel vision every now and again by taking in my surroundings. Definitely getting rural now as we head towards Ashford. Traffic has thinned and the quality and width of the pavement tells me very few folks use it! The broken surface is not helping me but I'm buggered: running in the gutter on the road is out because I'm scared of prolonged periods on a camber, and running in the middle of the road is out because - well, it's not very sensible. And this is the routine for the next couple of miles: focus in, keep face, shoulders, arms and hands relaxed, stay smooth, keep rhythm, keep RUNNING. Look up, deep breaths, shake down, take in the sights - where's the van? - more deep breaths, then focus in...

But now I'm really starting to cook and feel tired as my mind starts to play tricks. I've been pretty good at estimating time / distance completed without using a watch - and I'm not wearing one - but as I think I'm nearing the 60 mile mark I start to pass a series of lay-bys on my left. To me, lay-bys only mean one thing: the motorhome parked up which means it's time for me to stop. So as I crest a particularly nasty short rise and the first lay-by appears, I'm looking eagerly for the van. I've slowed to a walk in anticipation of the stop, (I always walk the final stretch into and out of the stops) but no van. Bollocks. Oh well...but getting into a run is hard now. The van pulls up alongside from following me and Ed looks out: "Just down this road, Andy - just keep it going a while longer." A while longer. Well, OK if you say so.

The second lay-by: 'It's gotta be here - there's even a café - the boys will definitely have stopped by a café: 60 miles. Legs are ****ed, I'm a bit bushed, but I'm here - massage and food and I'll be OK.'

But there's no van - this is not the 60 mile point. Disbelief, confusion and disappointment momentarily swamp me. The shade of the trees ends, the open road starts again and no sign of the motorhome. I do stoic and get on with it - but the mental hurt is now as big as the physical.

Then there's the van parked on the verge - no motorhome: have they got lost? - but the van will do. As far as I am concerned this IS the 60 mile point. Ed gives me the good news: 'It's about a mile down the road - they're parked up waiting for us.'

You're having a ****ing laugh, I think - I'm not going anywhere. However, because I was brought up properly I make an attempt to do coherent and polite. 'I just need to get out of this heat and lie down for a bit. I'm a bit bollocked - can you get the van to come back here instead?' So while the boys get sorted I make a slow and painful attempt to lie down with legs raised in the back of the van. Closing my eyes in the shade is bliss - though I can feel my blood thumping through my body.

It's a longer-than-planned-for stop, but some damage has been done in that last section and I need a re-charge. Ten mile chunks are definitely far too long, and now it looks like five mile sections are pushing it. John has to take the longest time yet to work some range of movement and elasticity back into my legs. We have to be careful - any sudden movement will bring a yelp of pain. It's the first time I've stopped short of a planned marker and I know the crew will register what is the first real blip. I don't. In my head I'm 60 miles to the good. My quads are ****ed but everything else is fine and mentally I'm great. The treat foods come out and Charly takes time to relay some good will messages that have come in by phone. More evidence that this is a solo challenge in name only, and I'm quickly smiling and joking.

John is starting to get concerned though, and we talk damage limitation. "Are you using your arms much?" "Not really, I'm just trying to stay relaxed and smooth." "Maybe you should bring 'em in more". he suggests, "cos you've got to try and get your knees to lift again. Keep the knee lift and you help keep the muscle length. Everything's just tightening up at the moment and you're no better than shuffling." No kidding, I think, but I'm still ****ing running this thing.

Half an hour later I'm back on my feet but now it's a walk-shuffle-trot-run routine which I have to repeat a few times before I can make the running bit stick. I've asked for brief stop with the van at 2.5 miles and then a longer one with the motorhome at five miles. A few miles on and Ed runs with me for a few miles in the midday heat. We talk quietly about the challenge and share some memories as well as some hopes and fears. We even do a radio interview with one of the local stations. It all helps pass the miles and I'm definitely moving better.

Ashford and 65 miles and the crew keep the stop short. There is an air of urgency now: get him in, get sorted, and get out again: movement is good and static is death - so keep moving! On the couch in the shade, wipe down with baby wipes, cover head with wet cold towel, shoes and socks off, re-apply vaseline to feet, change socks, massage, shoes on - on yeah, and keep eating and drinking! Keep thinking GOOD THOUGHTS: you're getting there and everything's in the green.

Roadside assistance with John and Charly

John has decided to run with me for a couple of miles - essentially to bully me into picking my knees up and opening my stride. He wants to see for himself what's happening out here in the field. I'm into my running quicker this time, and I'm immediately aware the pace is faster. So be it. I fix on John's heels in front of me and work to keep with him. "Work your arms - pick your knees up! C'mon Andy, work through it - it'll get easier as you get into it!"

So I grit my teeth and work as my world shrinks to feature the point between John's shoulder blades and little else. We're on a shit camber, the road has narrowed, and traffic is once again brushing past us. I'm trying to do 'relaxed' and 'flow' through clenched teeth. I'm aware I'm working way harder than previously and now my shoulders are aching with the effort. "Just do it, man - don't think about it, just ****ing do it."

This time we don't stop after 2.5 miles. I try to remember that my world hasn't always revolved around chasing John's back, but this seems a pointless waste of mental energy: let's keep it in the present, shall we?

2pm and I collapse on the couch where the motorhome is parked up in a village hall car park. I'm breathing hard, in real pain and just want to sleep. John has run on ahead to get ready for me and tests a drinks bottle Charlotte has ready: "That's no good, it's bloody warm - he needs something cold!" It's the first raised voice of the trip and reflects the urgency and concern John in particular feels as he works quickly to get to grips with my legs. Too quickly: his grip slips on my ankle, he falls forward onto me, my knee goes through full range of motion and I scream as the quad muscle is forced to full stretch. Jesus ****ing Christ!! I've tears in my eyes as I'm wrenched from the twilight zone into full wakefulness. John is suitably chaste, we all take a deep breath and settle down.

"I think that's 75 miles, Andy." Really? Where did that last few miles go then - I'm sure I've not lost track that badly - have I? 75 miles. Wow - that's close: I can almost touch it...

"Let me check that," says Eddie. "It may not be: let me check it." He knows that because of the detours the van made through London, the clock mileage in the van is slightly more that I have actually covered.

"Andy, that's 70 miles: 70 miles, buddy. Well done."

70 miles. I thought 75 sounded a bit far. Still, only 15 and a bit to go. I allow myself a smile as the crew go into serious pamper-mode. John is still working to keep the stops short: Charly is assisting with foot massage and vaseline while multi-tasking with food and text messages and EVERYONE is making a real effort to keep conversation going and talk the achievement UP: silences are not helpful right now.

After half an hour I'm off walking again still with John for company. I walk fast and try repeatedly to break into a jog but my legs are having none of it. This is ****ing crazy - COME ON YOU BASTARD - RUN! You can move so you can run - come ON! Through silent tears of frustration which are fortunately indistinguishable from sweat I eventually force myself into a parody of a run - but it's NOT walking and that's ALL that matters.

It still feels fast though as John continues to run ahead checking over his shoulder periodically. My world has reverted to the familiar but now it's even smaller. I'm pretty much ignoring John, letting his exhortations pass through me, and just concentrating on MOVING FORWARD.

And then we pass the first sign I can remember with Folkestone on it. Folkestone's near Dover, isn't it? John's clearly delighted and I grimace in what passes for a smile in response. It's getting harder to keep running and I am reduced to a walk on the broken, narrow and overgrown pavement sections before cursing myself into running once again. Part of me is aware that a few red lights are starting to flash, and that part is trying to get the attention of the other part. F*** off - can't you see I'm busy here?

Then the van comes into view and I wobble gratefully down the slight dip, stop, sway - and would have fallen if Ed had been less aware. He is able to catch me and lowers me into the shade at the back of the van as I'm finally forced to pay attention to those flashing red lights...Shit. This is definitely not good.

I'm now paying for those last miles with John with interest, and for a few minutes feelings of failure and frustration and helplessness overwhelm me. I can't stop the tears as I try to explain to Ed how I feel and why I'm crying. I'm still emotional when after some drink and fruit I set off walking again this time with Ed for company. I get it together fairly quickly after that though and Ed goes on ahead to leave me to walk the couple of miles or so to the motorhome at 75 miles. By the time I reach the crew again I'm composed and am walking strongly - but it doesn't last.

Once on the couch again surrounded by the guys the façade shatters. I have realised in the last mile or so that I CANNOT run any further. It's got nothing to do with anything else except that my quadricep muscles are shot and I physically cannot lift my knees any more. Feelings of failure and frustration simply swallow me: Seeing Charlotte tips me over the edge - I can't look her in the eyes so bury my head in the couch and cry my eyes out. She reaches for my hand and I know she's crying with me. A small part of me has registered that everyone else has backed off and Tim is no longer filming.

"Babe." I raise my gaze and we smile at each other through the tears. "What's wrong - you've done great: you're doing SO well..." I realise she doesn't get it so try and explain. "I'm OK - everything's OK, it's just my legs: my quads are ****ed and I can't run - I just can't!"

"So just walk for a bit and see how you feel."

She still doesn't get it.

"But it's RUN - I wanted to run it: I just wanted to run the whole thing, that's all...and now I can't...I just can't..."

She smiles broadly as she quickly realises there's no major problems: "Ohhh...is that all! Look everyone, he's human after all - Andy's human!"

And perspective comes quickly after that. I need to change some shit, but as Eddie C points out, I'm actually walking faster than those last few running miles and the main goal IS to get to Dover in one piece. I'm still well up on record pace and have got just over 10 miles to go. I know from the last mile or so I can walk strongly, my feet are fine and I'm so close now I can almost taste it.

If walking is all I have left then I'll ****ing walk the rest of the way.

From Eddie's log: *80 miles on the van clock Andy arrives at the camper 3.31pm. He had a couple of wobbly moments during the last four miles but recovered well as he walked on. He had a few tears when we talked, but all in all seemed OK.*

He is now laid on the bed being well looked after. The afternoon sun has been very hot. That has played its part.

I phoned the skipper of the boat and he has told me he will call when he has the weather report. I said there is no way Andy will not swim tomorrow, but he (the skipper) did not seem so confident.

At the massage table all around Andy praising him and boosting his confidence. He recovers quickly once he stops.

3.46pm and he is getting ready to leave. The decision has been made to walk instead of run to the next target: the walk looks good and strong - the determination is back.

I reach Dover and the end of the first stage at 7.10pm after walking the rest of the way: 18.5 hours since I left London. In my heart of hearts it's all a little later than I wanted, but I'm HERE which is the primary aim and I'll take that. The walk in has been interesting in its own way: I've had to walk backwards down one particularly short steep hill - the only way my legs could cope - we've had traffic hailing us as a result of local radio coverage we've had, and Chris our pilot for the swim has come out to meet us in advance of tomorrow. There are two swim windows: the first in the early hours of the morning and the second at midday. It's my call and I only briefly consider the first. We're up on schedule, I'm out on my feet, and I need to repair the damage - so it's midday tomorrow.

I'm not sure who is proudest: with Eddie at the end of the run

There are hugs and handshakes all around as we do the obligatory photos bit at the end of the run.

I move with all the grace of an arthritic octogenarian into the motor home.

"Ahh, it's nice to stop - what time is it?"

"7 o'clock - you've only been about 19 hours: NINETEEN hours - that's endurance, man!" John shakes his head in admiration.

"A little less, actually," corrects Charlotte. "It's more like 18 and a half."

"18 and a half..." I'm a little slow as the effort of speaking is almost too much now. "Well, I couldn't go any quicker..."

The guys are quick to pour cold water on that one,

Charlotte: "You flew!"

John : "It was brilliant!"

Charlotte: "Could you not? Really?!"

John: "Perhaps the next time you'll be a bit quicker now you've got the hang on it!"

I give in and have to smile. "Yeah - just a bit of a trial run, that..."

I realise that I am absolutely shattered, and once the smiles stop it's all I can do to keep my eyes open. The urge to just STOP, close my eyes and just lie down is nearly overwhelming, and the guys have to physically prop me up and steer me into our B & B for the night. Thankfully it's a ground floor room - but there is no bath! I can barely bend so the prospect of a shower is seriously daunting but somehow I manage. John comes in to do his stuff on my legs once again and we send out for ice-bags to speed the recovery. Apart from the traumatised quads I realise that I'm in quite serious pain in my right hip as well. The bursae is seriously inflamed to the point where I can hardly move: I definitely don't want to take this into the swim with me.

The boys are sorting themselves out but Charly and I are not going anywhere and eating in is the only option. She is shattered herself and is nearly reduced to tears after futile attempts to get some sort of takeaway food delivered to the B & B. I can barely string a coherent sentence together so she is forced to get this sorted herself and in the end has to go back out and buy a pasta takeaway to bring back. In the meantime I have fallen asleep and she has to wake me to eat. Barely has the last mouthful passed my lips and I'm out once again for the count and sleep like a dead thing all the way through to morning.

Someone once said that training is physical but performance is emotional - much more about heart and soul. If it matters it will therefore hurt to fall short - and all the 72 mile point illustrated was that IT REALLY MATTERED to be able to run the whole damn way. If you go back to how I set this up, the quality of the journey is AS important as the outcome: so my private goal - the one closest to my heart - had to be to commit to try. I didn't know if I could but there really was only one way to find out.

But there was always something to grab a hold of. Multiple goals on many different levels and all within the various bite-size chunks meant that there was always some achievement to celebrate - and this was key in maintaining momentum. The pit-stops were also an opportunity to reflect and with time comes perspective - and I didn't need long. Physically I was in great shape so the physical recovery was fast, and we'd also set the stops up to maximise ALL aspects of the recovery: physical, mental and emotional. As Eddie noted in his log - I recover well when I stop. Mental rehearsal during the training meant that I'd worked on anticipating as many different scenarios as possible and was able to see myself dealing with each of them: the result? Not much took me by surprise!

The bottom line? Just get to Dover - and do it without killing yourself. In this context then the strategy was straightforward: not getting the result I wanted? Learn from that QUICKLY and change the approach - but then get back on the horse and stay with it. Remember the Goal, the WHY of all of this and how far you've come already.

You must do that which you think you cannot.

Footnote: Andy went on to reach Paris and complete the A2A Challenge becoming only the second person to do so. His fastest stage times still stand today (Dec 2011). You can read the full story in his book *London To Paris The Hard Way*.

2004

The first 'life after triathlon' year.

Business is going well, I'm working round the country and in Europe, Charly and I had been married two years - we have no ties and it feels like money to burn!

Arch To Arc is still very fresh as I'm now on the writing and 'making sense of it' stage.

I'd stopped swim training in autumn 2003 after failing to get my head around swimming pools after my Enduroman Arch To Arc triathlon. Still biking, but needing something to fill the void. That something was ultra running and this year saw three: 33 miles at Marlborough Downs in May, my first foray into the six day stage race format at Marathon of Britain in July, and 40 miles at High Peak in September. I ran well in all three, and still easily recall flying along by the canal at six minute mile pace at around the 18 mile mark at Marlborough. I was even training on the track during the summer - happy days!

Marathon of Britain 2004: The Joy of Six

175 miles, 6 Days

Missed your train or car run out of petrol? Need to get to Nottingham from Worcester? No worries - the Good Lord gave you feet, didn't he? He surely did, though I can safely say they've never been subjected to 175 miles of footpaths in the space of a week before!

Marathon of Britain took place for the first time in 2003, and is the brainchild of ultra-dude Rory Coleman, recently returned from running from London to Lisbon - as you do. Modelled on the famous Marathon de Sables, it retains the format but not the sand dunes. The UK version links Worcester and Nottingham by footpath over six days with an emphasis on navigation, self-sufficiency and an ability to last the course. You are fed at the start and the end of the day, housed in communal tents, but apart from that you carry everything you need for six days.

I first heard about it in the spring, and as I had a bit of a hole in my diary when compared to last year (!) I thought, 'what the heck' and signed up. The route itself looked fabulous, winding its way through the sweet spots of Middle England, so if the weather was with us I figured we would at least be in for some spectacular scenery. In that at least, we were not disappointed.

I realised pretty quick that I had very little idea of exactly what I'd taken on. OK, I'd done endurance stuff over three days, but that was multi-sport which at least spreads the effort. This was a single sport over SIX days! I remembered how I felt 72 miles from London last year when my running legs gave out - now I'd committed to more than DOUBLE the distance. Time to start filling in the blanks then...

A Few Thoughts On Method

Now I thought this whole thing was pretty cool and sufficiently out of my comfort zone to get my attention, but I had to do my own thing. That meant not being aware of stage times and not looking at the results list all week. Ignore the thing and don't listen when other people were talking about it!

The ole competitive juices wouldn't quite lie down though. I knew last year's winner was entered again, so I resolved to run with him for at least part of stage one to see how fast he went and how he did it. I'd heard he wasn't too hot on the navigating, but as record holder for Land's End to John O'Groats, (9 days something covering over 85 miles per 24 hours) Andy Rivitt obviously knew something about being on his feet! I also knew I'd learned a truck load about this stuff as well since last year, and I also knew that I could do recovery and perseverance really bloody well.

Stage five would be the longest stage by a big margin. My strategy was to get to the start of this intact and without killing myself. I figured more people than not would struggle on that stage. My plan was to be part of the few that did not.

Then there were ways in which I could support myself during the preparation and the event itself. The priorities I had. How I chose to spend my time. What I said to myself. What I believed about the event and my abilities.

Everything breaks down into bite-size chunks. And the whole thing? In my head it was never 175 miles. At its very simplistic level that was just time on my feet - all I had to do was to keep moving. Take it stage by stage and page by page on our Route Book.. Don't think about the whole thing - then break each stage down as well: checkpoint to checkpoint, and smaller than that if I need to. Perseverance and recovery would be the glue to hold the chunks together.

I trawled the web ultra-running chat rooms, the MOB web forum, read, researched, spent time with mad ultra-folks, then tried the stuff out myself. The real test is whether you can maintain this focus when things go wrong.

This was the situation I faced week five of the six week prep period I'd allocated myself. I'd over-trained and picked up an injury. I'd been training differently - running with a rucksac filled with medicine balls and building up to running twice a day with quality runs over a block of three consecutive days. In the end it was too much. Week five was therefore spent focusing on being a model patient and doing everything I could to speed the recovery. It worked, and with five days to go I was running easy and pain-free again - but it was a test.

Why does a pre-race taper work? 'Cos this is when the body adapts best from the training.' Same principle here: This is when the real learning happens - the trick is to plan it in as a priority and not leave it to chance. So I kept a diary during the event. After each stage the guys got used to seeing me scribble away. It helped keep perspective, reflect honestly and learn from the events of the day. That helped me feel good about myself and THAT was damn useful when you've got 175 miles to cover!

I took a mat to sleep on. Many folks didn't want the weight - but I knew I'd need to maximise my chances to rest! I also had little treats and habits to maximise the impact of the recovery time. I took sachets of cool-gel to use during my post-stage self massage. I showered after each stage. (six days sleeping in a field and getting very sweaty and run down was a great way to pick up infections and exacerbate any foot problems).

Personal hygiene I felt was going to be a real issue. There were no showers or hot water but there were plenty of bottles of drinking water. So I used to grab a fistful of these, got my bits out and got on with it. And guess what, I FELT better afterwards! Because we had to carry everything we would need for six days, weight was a premium. Many folks just didn't bring wash kit etc. Their choice - but more people looked and felt crap by the end of the week than didn't - and I saw some feet in states you wouldn't believe!).

A jelly-baby every time I turned a page of the Route Book made me smile. Another food treat and a healthy dose of positive self-talk at every checkpoint. Paying attention to the view as we went along - it was a stunning route in places - and then every time the next step and the next step, knowing that it was all bringing me closer to The End.

Stage 1: 16 miles / three Checkpoints Malvern Town Centre to Croome Country Park

Straight up to Malvern Beacon, along the ridgeline of the hills then drop down and head NE for Croome. Thirty-eight started in glorious weather which soon narrowed down to about five of us going flat out for the Beacon. Nice steady pace? No chance - this was flat out fellracing with 174 miles to go! This soon got everyone spread out as there were all shapes and sizes and abilities here. Everyone from the racing snakes at the front to folks who were walking the whole thing at 3-4 mph. (I later figured out that those racing at the head of the field from last year were running to a simple tactic: work hard to establish a gap on Day One - then protect that gap. Me, I was just out for a jolly at that point...)

But I did want to get close to last year's winner on this stage to have a look and see how fast he ran. I'd heard he wasn't too hot with a map - and I was right! - but he was here last year so did have that advantage. By the time we got off the hills a loose group of about 3-4 of us were away. A couple of dodgy map moments trying to find footpaths through and around fields in various combinations split us up and the heat over the last five miles did its work too.

Despite having to use my emergency jelly babies in the last miles I trotted in 2nd place about 10 minutes behind Andy R who had blitzed the stage over 10 minutes faster than he ran it last year. One down, five to go and loads of lessons in the process.

Stage 2: 29 miles / 5 Checkpoints Croome to Broadway

After a second night under canvas most of us are still sleeping crap - not tired enough yet to sleep on and through anything! The other change is that today our legs are also hurting - and I realise belatedly that descending like a lunatic off Malvern Beacon probably wasn't such a smart move after all! So it is a much steadier start with the field pretty much together for the first flat few miles. Today however, is the BIG HILLY day: four big climbs including a fearsome one to finish up to Broadway Tower. It's also blazingly hot. The first climb takes us onto Bredon Hill for stunning views across the Cotswolds.

Hanno, one of the German contingent has set his heart on a stage win today and is pushing on ahead using the most awkward style imaginable - but it's deceptively fast! We let him go and I focus on keeping it all under control. It's hotter than a snake's ass out here. The day is not without drama with the only two retirements of the whole week. One of them is last year's winner who collapses at halfway. He is fortunately found soon after but it's a close call and he's whisked to hospital a very lucky bunny.

I decide to take a detour round the local Coop in Broadway to stock up on food, so trade calories for time: I figure it's a good deal and finish tired but OK at the end of a day which has wreaked havoc on the field. The evening clinic with our two race doctors is very popular and very vocal. The best treatment for blisters is simple and ruthless - particularly if you want to run on 'em the following day. The routine was perfected during last year: lance 'em with a scalpel, drain 'em, flush 'em with iodine, and pad and strap 'em My trusty plates of meat are standing up well, so those of us who are affliction-free sit back and listen to the screams rending the evening air..

Stage 3: 33 miles / 5 Checkpoints Broadway to Stratford Racecourse

Definitely sore pins today and very much damper after a couple of huge thunderstorms yesterday evening. One of last year's top finishers makes a break early on, and I think 'sod it - let's cover it!'

So the first few miles are fast till we all settle down again. Then the biggest map-reading error costs a group of three of us about 15 minutes and to add insult to injury I hit a bad patch and grovel about pathetically for a few miles as we wind our way to Long Marston and the start of the Greenway and the long run into Stratford. I pick up, hook up with Sammy the Squaddie and positively fly down towards Stratford making up chunks of time and distance.

Then the cruel bit: We run right past the finish and onto a 10 mile loop which will bring us back on ourselves. But it's all very strong stuff, and Sammy and I continue to push and we finish strongly only a few minutes down on the stage winner. Not long after the heavens open and we get the mother of all storms to really test the tents and the morale of the rest of the MOB field yet to finish. Spirits are strong though, and everyone makes it in over the next few hours very bedraggled but delighted to get here.

Stage 4: 35 miles / 4 Checkpoints Stratford to Coombe Abbey Country Park

Perversely, my pins feel better today! So clearly, three days to 'bed in' then it's just a normal day, huh?! I'm planning another big food stop today at about a third distance in Warwick. Again, I figure the calories for time trade is worth it. We pass the 100 mile point at Kenilworth Castle - hurrah!

But I really struggle over the next few miles and have to curse myself into keeping moving. I realise belatedly that I'm simply overheating, and swapping a T shirt for my usual vest does the trick. I'm not out of the woods yet though, and can feel all is not well under my left foot. There's little I can do except finish and sort it out then, but now I'm worried as my plan of getting to the start of the BIG DAY intact is going out the window. It is today that eventual MOB 2004 winner Jez Bragg puts the race away: he simply runs away with the stage and puts nearly 45 mins on the second place finisher. Not bad for a young man in his twenties with only a few years' running in him.

I walk the last few miles tired and hobbling but pleased to limit the damage as my 'bad' day is still relatively good. But it's my turn to scream later as the doc has to do some serious scalpel and iodine work to the sole of my foot. I really thought I could 'do' pain, but this is really something else - but so is the risk of infection. We pad and strap it and I leave wondering how the heck I will do 55 miles on it tomorrow over rough terrain. Ah well, let's figure that out in the morning.

Stage 5: 55 miles / 6 Checkpoints Coventry to Soar Valley Meadows

Today is THE DAY. I figured that more people will struggle today than go well. I had not put myself in a box up to now because I wanted to get to this point in relatively good shape. The legs feel OK but I need to take my traumatised foot for a spin. Remarkably a few test-jogs prove that the pads and straps are doing their job - and I'm soon grinning like a loon: LET'S GET IT ON!

It will be another baking hot day. The folks at the back of the field have set off at 4.30am and 7am. It is estimated that some of them will take over 24 hours for the stage - and at the front of the field we will probably pass some of them at about a third distance. These are the real heroes.

Through Wolvey and we are soon on the canal heading for Hinckley. All very familiar stuff now as we head by the water towards Market Bosworth. I'm working with a new tactic today: my watch set to bleep every hour to remind me to eat - no chances taken today. Our lead group splits along this stretch and we start to pass the back markers. We have all got to know each other pretty well over the past days and there is a huge sense of camaraderie. We know an awful lot of folks are in for a very long day, so take time to wish them well.

I'm cruising along quite happily on my own by Bosworth and scare the customers of a local cake shop by breezing in and dripping all over the counter! Then it's over the fields on the Leicester Round to Markfield and Bradgate. I catch one of the early leaders and hit Bradgate feeling great! I've promised myself I'll call Charlotte on my mobile when I get to the Old John landmark - as at that point I will be able to see the power station which is the stage finish. I'm 10 minutes down on the three leaders so decide to push hard over this next section into Lough-boro' putting my local knowledge to use: I want to catch and pass 'em!

A breathless call to my wife catches her right out and my spirits stay high as I work hard to the 45 mile point along the canal in Loughboro'. Two minutes! I get a time check, and sure enough in the distance I can make out a familiar figure. I throw my trusty mental lasso and pull, but then clear of Loughboro' heading up the river to Kegworth the lasso breaks. I grind to a halt: I have simply pushed too fast too soon. Oh, well, back to Plan B: Just Keep Moving! So I walk and eat and drink try-ing to get the energy back up. We are on a section broken with fences and stiles so I do a deal with myself: walk a section, run a section all the way to Kegworth. This works for a while, but I find it difficult to keep my spirits up on this endless stretch of river: where the **** is Kegworth?!

Then the mother of all storms drops on us: Thunder, lightning - the lot. I can barely see straight never mind anything else. My spirits plummet and I just get my head down and stomp in a fearful temper along the path, swearing and cursing my head off at everything and nothing. Oh dear - but at least I'm moving.

Having a sense of humour failure in the storm

The last checkpoint means I'm about three miles away. I curse myself into a run as the storm continues to wreak havoc around us. The final stretch seems endless but finally I see the glow of floodlights in the camp, and I'm in. Thank f*** for that!

Stage 6: 10 miles / 1 Checkpoint Soar Valley Meadows to Nottingham Castle

Throughout the night people have been finishing in various states. Hardly anyone sleeps. Those of us who are in, find ourselves helping those who stagger into our communal tents.

The defining moment of the whole week comes at 7.30am. Some 27 hours after starting the stage, Big Dave and Yogi walk into camp after going all night through the storm Yogi is in this for a bet, looks like shit and just keels over across the line. Dave is built like a brick shit-house, has walked over 500 marathons, but even he looks a little jaded. The rest of us just stand, stare, and applaud in absolute awe: Some are crying - all of us have a lump in our throat.

Two hours later they are on their feet again for the last 10 miles. Well, what the hell else would you do?

For the rest of us, the final stage is completed in a variety of ways. For me, that meant a steady wind up for the first five miles to break away, threshold for three miles to try and keep it, then a ferocious battle with Jez in the last few miles. 175 miles ends with a flat out sprint up to the Castle to just about throw up over the finish line! Jez wins the stage by a whisker and the race by at least eight miles. Unheard of before this week, Jez Bragg has arrived.

The things you do for fun, huh?

2005-2006

Two years without a diary and for the life of me I cannot recall why. I found some reference in my 2007 diary to 'apathy and injury the year before' so clearly - apart from Western States 100 - I was having a serious cave moment.

What I do know is that these were the peak business years of the decade for me. Charlotte and I had our separate careers and we collaborated regularly on 'Doing Big & Scary' matters. I was travelling and working lots, and then in late summer 2006 after a looooong time trying, Charly became pregnant. That triggered a 'so where do we want to raise a family?' discussion which resulted in a decision to move Up North. In autumn 2006 we put the house up for sale.

Our trip to the USA was a first - and what an event to start with. WS is the most prestigious 100 in the US and one of the very top races of its kind in the world - and I was Mr Green going into it. I knew I was physically under-prepared, but I believed I had what it took to reach the finish line. I was, and I had, but boy was it close.

Western States 100 2006:
Falling Down & Falling Short

100 miles - Two Feet - One Day

4.59am June 25th Squaw Valley, California, USA

Very nervous and trying to hide it with less than 16 minutes to go before the start

"One minute to go!" the PA blares. Charly and I have been wrapped in a hug standing at the edge of the assembled throng as runners disengage from loved ones and move to the start line. 380 runners from all over the world for arguably the most prestigious 100 of them all. 80's rock music blasts out and floodlights illuminate the first few hundred yards up the ski track. Straight up a 2500 foot climb to a ski station at the high point of the race at 8700 feet. Part of me smiles wryly at the lack of haste to get to the start: I will walk this climb and I don't care if I'm at the back!

It's one of those husband-wife moments. The magnitude of what we are about to do is starting to hit. The hug tightens and bottom lips begin to wobble. Some last kisses and searching glances, "I love you." Charly is as misty eyed as me, but I'm also a practical bloke: "Look after yourself, babe." Rest and food will be as important for her as for me, and though we've planned this as best we can she will have two things to contend with that I will not: waiting and worrying.

A last squeeze for my favourite lady and a smiling "I love you!" and then it's into the throng. Seconds to go and the countdown starts. '10, 9, 8...'

The front line sprints away into the predawn light.

Watching the Dawn

Climbing, climbing. Climbing. The track has wound its way through rock and snow steadily up switchbacks for the first few miles. After the mad rush of the start - I was pretty much at the back - the field settles and I'm walking strongly and passing people. Charly and I have been here for three days and we've noticed the altitude: Squaw Valley is at 6200' and I'm more breathless than normal. (Just how breathless I found out during a local bikram yoga class two days ago: very hot and a little bit bothered, I had a keeling over moment!)

I'm trying to watch the dawn breaking over the mountains behind me. I've got a small camera with me to capture those Kodak moments while on the move and I'm still sane - and this is definitely one of those. Oranges brighten to yellows as the sun emerges. 'Gonna be a warm one, then...'

As the first 25 miles unravel I'm accused of being from Texas and Wales and converse with varying degrees of accuracy and humour about English Royalty, the Boston Tea Party, and S&M to name but a few topics!

The running comes easily. Snow is still thick on the ground in many places as we are still around 7000' but while many are slipping, my trusty aggressive soles are doing their stuff and allowing me to skip daintily past. I figure enjoy it while you can!

Flowing Through Forests

Descending through these early pine forest is a foretaste of the key characteristic of this course: there is more down hill than uphill. I focus on smooth and easy descending but this still means I'm moving faster than most people around me. Is this still too fast? Will I pay for this later ? But it feels soooo easy!

The forests are so quiet that I feel I am obliged to tip-toe through them. I focus on doing just this and enjoy the fact that we are all starting to spread out now. I chat easily with people I catch and run with them for a while. I'm steadily making up ground but know that it is still all very early days - but it feels so easy...

Robinson Flat Aid Station

Relax. Flow. Walk the uphills. Smile. Chat with the aid station volunteers and remember your 'please' and 'thank yous'. Keep your head up and look around you - enjoy!

Down, down and down through the snowfields and the forests. The climbs are small but the descents are huge by comparison demanding discipline and concentration. Jamie the Kiwi and I find each other around the 20 mile point, and once we'd established an overseas connection it all just starts to flow between us. He's tall, lean and angular with the look of an outdoorsman: we quickly establish that we can both do dry humour very well - which is fine except much of it requires translating to our transient American audience!

Robinson Flat

The first big aid station at about 25 miles and the previous three have warmed me up to the way our US hosts do 'hosting!' This race has a great reputation for looking after the runners - 1400 volunteers for 380 runners makes for a great ratio!

It all starts a few hundred yards out from the aid station proper: A volunteer in radio contact with base giving a 'heads-up'. Quite often kids have come out to take our drinks bottles for a refill - and they run on ahead to do that for us.

Hand-written signs appear along the trail announcing the imminent oasis. Many stations are themed with volunteers in fancy dress, so everything is personalised accordingly. There's usually music and always someone to greet incoming runners. Their job is to welcome, establish initial needs and hand us off to our personal gofer for the duration of our stay. I will forever remember the 50-something lady who greeted me at the Devil's Thumb station at around halfway with the words, "Hi - I'm your personal slave!" I just had to ask her to repeat it slower so I could savour it!

Nothing is too much trouble and they appear to be able to provide everything! I thought I'd finally got one crew during the night at around 70 miles when they gave me some Coca-Cola - so I asked for Pepsi just for the hell of it. No such luck: a bottle of the rival brand was triumphantly produced - they were most put out when I had to admit I was just kidding!

Fruit, cold potatoes, turkey and jelly sandwiches, peanut butter sandwiches, crisps and pretzels, energy gels, water, coke, electrolyte replacement drink, sweets, cake and soup and noodles during the night. I'd have killed for a cup of tea, but when in the US...

It was hospitality with a big 'H' - and sometimes even too much. In the heat of the day, drinks would all be filled with ice including our bottle replenishment. I was leaving the aid stations shivering and it took me a while to figure out why and even my bottle was too cold to hold. After that it was definitely 'hold the ice, please!'

I just wasn't over-heating: the day temperature was in the 80s - cool for the time of year.

Robinson Flat was the first chance for support crews to meet their runners and Charly and I had arranged our first rendezvous here. The race was operating a 'park-and-ride' bus system as access to this remote station for cars was limited and the heavy snows had made this even more of an issue. We figured it'd be a bit of a bun-fight for crews. With this in mind, Charly had shot off from the start in our shiny rental SUV to get as close as she could - knowing that over 300 other crews would have the same idea! We'd tried to pack and label everything as smartly as possible, but she'd still have to carry kit for us both along trails to the aid station proper. (And you thought it was just me doing the endurance gig, huh?)

Insight: You can plan and prepack all you want re the food and drink needs. The only certainty is that at some point your runner will not want anything you've prepared, will not be able to offer any ideas as to what they do want - but hey, that sandwich you're eating looks nice..!

So Robinson Flat is a biggie: Jamie is also meeting Eileen his wife, and as we approach the crowds and noise become obvious. People are everywhere - shouting instructions, cheering: lots of 'Great job!' and waving. After the peace of the forest it's quite a change!

Someone takes my bumbag and I'm on the scales for the first time. The race organisation will do this four times today to keep an eye on the condition of the runners. '165 - what's your start weight?' I'm asked. I check the detail on my wristband where this an other vital stats are recorded. '163.' So I've gained 2lbs over this first section. Hmm...then I remember that last year's winning lady gained 9lbs over the first 50 miles: I figure I can live with two - it's the reduction in body weight the medical staff are watching for: 3% means significant dehydration, 5% is getting very silly, and 7%...you're probably going home in a van!

At the food table I'm momentarily at a loss as to what to choose: the choices! The volunteers are asking questions but I'm just doing 'overwhelmed' right now! I belatedly realise that this is one of the downsides of not having a fixed plan - Charly and I have sketched in the basics but that's all. 'Er...' I grab some electrolyte replacement and then remember I've got a small plastic 'doggy-bag' for just this purpose - so I proceed to fill it with goodies: I can eat on the trail - but I need another pair of hands, though! Then out and through the lines of cheering people scanning for my wife - who is waving frantically to get my attention.

Smile, kiss, hug: "Hi Babe!" We walk a few yards to where she has stashed our kit, swapping news. I'm fine, feel easy, no worries. She's had a bit more of a fight to get here and has traded sleep time for a big breakfast. I'm pleased. 'Sock change?' Yeah. We proceed to do a really good impression of playing 'Twister' before I remember that we'd said we should do this with me on my back so we can wipe, dry and massage my feet easily. Too late - and there's no space for it anyway. Charly pulls a face. "Yeah, I know - we'll sort it out for next time, OK?" OK.

I grab some replacement food of cold pizza, pretzels, fig rolls and a kiwi fruit to go with my existing picnic. It all feels a bit more chaotic that I would like, but I've only got myself to blame for this. There's 'roll with it' and 'plan for it'. Y'all can't have both!

Still, I'm in and out pretty sharpish as the next checkpoint is only three miles away and Charly will drive ahead and meet me again - a real treat! Despite a less than polished routine all is in the green, and I'm off walking and eating. Jamie and I find each other again before I'm forced to make my first pit-stop. So peanut butter and fig rolls don't agree with me then...

Downs & Ups

The 30-56 mile section is the one which really stood out on the race profile chart. We are now entering the canyons, and the switchback descents range from 2,500 - 2000 feet and we climb straight back out for 1500-1800 feet. Three canyons. Three times. This is the real Quad Killer. Little did I know that this would also be the Toe Killer...

The 56 mile aid station at Michigan Bluff is the next biggie and where I'll next see Charly. I know that it is imperative I get to this in good shape.

The First Cracks Appear

Jamie is struggling. Though much of the course is now shaded we are in the heat of the day. Walk the climbs, run the descents and as much of the flats as you can. It's hot and we've two canyons to go. Running easily through beautiful forest I'm enjoying the sights and sounds when, "You go on, Andy." Jamie is labouring and has dropped to a walk. I hesitate briefly then turn round. "Bollocks to that! I'm OK - let's just gear it down for the next bit: we're doing good - still catching people - just keep it steady, OK?"

This is the pattern for the next few miles: short sections of walking and jogging and talking to Jamie almost constantly: "Walk a bit, Jamie, run from this next tree, keep it steady, every step gets us closer, we're doing great - just keep doing it, man!"

And we do it. Down the endless switchbacks which go on and on and on. Stay smooth, don't hammer it, walk if it gets too steep, across the river bridge at the bottom then walk - hands on knees up and up and up. I vary my climbing style: Sometimes short upright steps, some-times long bent forward strides in order to vary the load on the legs. I smile to myself that possibly a few repetitions up and down Croft Hill and Bradgate Park might just not be enough for this! I put my faith in my weight training but know that only time will tell...

I get the first signs on the last descent: soreness in both big toes. It feels like I'm losing both toenails from the unrelenting pressure on the front of the feet. The pain quickly escalates over the next few miles till any trip or stubbed toe brings a sharp intake of breath - or a yelp of pain. I grimace but say nothing as the damage was probably done right at the start with the choice of a thicker set of socks - and with hindsight I needed toe-box room more. I guess we'll find out at Michigan...

On the final climb in this section the tables turn and it's now me who is following. It's murderously steep and for the first time I'm strug-gling to stay with Jamie. He opens a gap of 10 yards and I'm gritting my teeth to keep it at 10 as my breathing rate spirals higher for the first time: guess this is where the fun starts. His watch bleeps: "That's 12 hours, Andy!" Bloody hell! Where did the day go? I'm genuinely shocked at the time as I've been oblivious to the passing of the hours: I've not been watching the position of the sun - I'm not wearing a watch as usual. But neither do I attach any significance to this as I do not have any time-dependent goals. Jamie has, however. 'I'd hoped to be at MB by now, 'he says over his shoulder. I do a quick calculation: we've passed the checkpoint prior to MB which I recall is only a few miles away from MB itself. "Yeah, but we'll be close", I reply, "We're not a million miles away, and I'm just damn pleased to get here!"

Jamie grins back: "Me too, sport - your plans here?"

"A shoe change, eat, drink, feet up and chill a bit with Charly." I also want to have a look at the toe damage but figure a change to older, roomier trainers will help anyway. "Maybe 10-15 minutes. You fancy staying together for the next bit?"

"Sounds good," comes the reply. "I've got my shoe change at Foresthill, (62 miles) and I'm also picking up my pacer…"

A Few Words On Pacers

The race offered those who wanted it a chance to 'pair up' for the final 40 miles or so - the pacers are usually local runners who know the trails. I've never contemplated one before and didn't give this much thought pre-race. Now, after 56 miles or so I can see the value of experienced company going into the night section. Still…

Michigan Bluff

The aid station explodes at us in a deluge of sight and sound we have been without for the last five hours or so - there's hundreds of people here!

I'm delighted to be here, albeit with sore feet but otherwise in good spirits: 56 miles to the good and still in control of my faculties.

Onto the scales and this time I've lost weight. Okayyyy. I reassure the volunteers that I'm about to pig out and they let me go without too much fuss.

This time Charly has found a spot where we can spread out.

I gain huge points with the watching crowd by presenting my favourite lady with a flower I swiped on the way in. She grins happily and puts it behind her ear. I'm delighted to see her and while we try to out-grin each other Jamie introduces us to his wife Eileen - so some company for Charly for the next section as well!

I lie down and start to do the foot thing while Charly digs out the goodies. She's even brought my special request hamburger - then surpasses that by producing a handful of strawberries and carrot sticks! Fruit and fresh stuff is a real treat! We swap news as she starts on the foot care and I start to eat...but then stop. After a few mouthfuls I suddenly don't want anything and cast around for something which I fancy eating. Nothing. You gotta eat, man. I know, but...

"Charly, any pasta?" We'd planned a cold pasta meal around now, but Charly looks momentarily crestfallen. "No, I haven't. I'm sorry... Oh. But I can get you some for Foresthill?" I perk up, "Great! - no worries. Can I have your sandwich, then?" You gotta eat, man...

With shoes off I inspect my soggy feet. Three toenails are black including both big ones, which also are very sore and swollen. It looks like the nails have been pushed back into the bed by all the descending. OK. We clean and re-vaseline them, and I switch to thinner socks and my older bigger trainers. I hope it will be enough. Other than that - no blisters.

You need to eat, man...

I know.

I shovel some food down and the rest into my picnic bag to eat en route. Charly is still clearly concerned and more so when she hears that I'm now losing weight - but promises macaroni cheese in seven miles.

Hey, but it's nice just to lie here for a bit...

"Andy, c'mon man - we've been here too long!"

A now familiar Kiwi twang rouses me.

7 miles. About 1.5 hours on the terrain we'll be on.

The Trail to Forresthill

So now the fun begins. Yesterday Charly and I sketched out a best-case scenario which would bring me home in about 20 hours - and we'd looked really hard at this to be sure. OK, I'd have to be going well, but four hours for 20 miles? That's possible, isn't it?

Sure. Just not over this course in the shape you are in today, my friend!

My dear wife knew that after the first quarter we were way too optimistic and has been adjusting since. I am not focused on time at all, so until Jamie's watch went off I'd no idea about pace. Time not withstanding, the goal was to get to MB in good shape, and feet aside - I figure I can pad 'em and strap 'em if I need to - I've achieved that.

While the course description told the story, it has taken actually doing it to appreciate the magnitude of the climbs and descents. I know I can walk four mph even on busted quads - as that was exactly what I did during my London to Paris jaunt - but that's on good terrain. On this stuff? Not even close!

The trail is well marked but it's all rocky singletrack: add a downhill in and it gets real interesting if one is trying to protect one's toes. Doing all this at night will be an experience to say the least!

Jamie is focused on a 24 hour finish. This is the four minute-mile equivalent on this course and we're on schedule - just. A 24 would be really cool as well, but I want to finish first and this time I don't want to have to put myself in a box to do it. WS is the benchmark test for me: Finish, take the experience and the learns and come back smarter. But a 24 would be nice...and I could do it.

Just hold up for this next section and see...

New Zealand In The Lead!

Jamie is definitely much stronger now and forges ahead on the climbs. I focus on holding the gap steady and running smooth with good form. As time goes on the tendency to lean forwards gets greater - we've already seen runners almost bent double - and I'm starting to get back ache from my own efforts. I keep the dark side at bay: much is in the green and we're moving well.

The Foresthill aid station is reached after a brute of a climb. It's not too long but I'm having to work harder than I want to to stay with the flying Kiwi. We're still chatting away and morale is good, but my damn legs just won't go as fast as I want 'em to! I have to focus really hard to override the slow cruise pace they seem to have acquired for themselves.

Charly has come out about half a mile from the aid station to meet us and while Jamie surges ahead for his own shoe change, I run with my fave lady. She says later that she knew something wasn't right. We catch up on news but I'm not exactly Mr Chatty.

Once we arrive my attention is all on not losing Jamie. Deep down I know that the next 20 miles are crucial and going solo into the night with deteriorating legs will be tough. If I can just hang onto Jamie and his pacer it will be so much easier. So I'm like a hound with a scent... Don't lose him, man!

Time to be weighed again and I'm still down by a few pounds - but this time I hide my wristband, lie about my starting weight so the loss appears less than it is, and reassure the folks that my wife has a big feed lined up for me - no way are you pulling me from this, sunshine!

"Pasta, Andy." Charly shoves a bowlful at me and I dig into it hungrily - only to nearly retch. Cold and congealed I can't swallow it down and hand it back. "Sorry, I'm sorry. I tried but..." I can see Charly fighting back tears - God knows how she's made time to cook this while on the move - but I just cannot stomach it. "It's OK, babe, it's OK: not a problem. What else have we got?"

I chuck down anything I can get my hands on but my attention is elsewhere...

"Where's Jamie? Did you see where he went?"

Charly points opposite us. "He's over there - look."

OK. Don't let him go. You have to stay with this.

"Andy. You need your night stuff." Charly pulls me back to Our Plan.

"You think I need it now?" It's still blazing sunshine and my time reckoning is all over the place, but Charly is right - it'll be dark before I reach the next big aid station and our next rendezvous.

Headtorch, spare batteries, spare long sleeved top, hat and waterproof are added to my load.

Charly wants to get my full attention but I'm completely focused on where Jamie is changing and am doing my own routine on automatic. She settles for helping with the practicals - but will say later that she regrets not confronting me at this point. She has learned that though I may be saying all the right things, if the eye contact isn't there then something is amiss. At mile 62 I am not focused on me for the first time: This is not good and I will pay for it later.

Are You Gonna Do This, Or What?

I'm up and ready before Jamie. Charly tries one last time: "See you at Green Gates (80m)." A hug and a kiss but it's too late. Jamie shoots off down the road with his pacer, a fresh pair of shoes and a whole sackful of re-charge! Within seconds I'm 20 yards adrift and dropping fast. Crunch time!

So Mounce, you can stick with 'em or let 'em go, but whatever you do you have to decide NOW. Make the choice!

No contest. I grimace, dig deep and eventually close up after 200 yards to say "Hi" to Matt the Pacer. I'm committed.

Matt wants to know our goals. "Finish in 24 hours," replies Jamie.

"What's more important?" asks Matt.

"Well...' Jamie gathers his thoughts. 'I'd like to finish first - and I want to finish with Andy."

I can see where this is going so jump in quick.

"Jamie, that's cool and it means a lot, but I don't want you to jeopardise a 24 hour finish by waiting for me!"

"It's not about that." Jamie is doing adamant. "You pulled me through the early bit and it doesn't feel right to finish any other way - I want us to finish together."

We argue respectfully back and forth, each juggling personal aspirations with obligations forged over spending the last 50 miles or so together.

I kill it: "Look. Let's get to the river crossing at 80 miles then we'll see."

That seems to do it - then Matt turns to me.

"What about you, Andy?" I toy briefly with sharing my own 24 hour aspirations but know my toes have been getting steadily worse and that descending is increasingly slow and painful. And this won't be improving.

"Hey - I'll be happy to finish, y'know?" And while that's true it's only part of the story. We're still on for a 24 and I'd be VERY happy with that, thank you...I just don't think my feet will let me.

"OK." Matt looks round. "I can keep us on schedule, but we need to run the downhills and as much of the flats as we can. Everyone ready? Let's go!"

Starting To Hurt

They say the race only really starts in the last third. A few hundred yards on we pass a lady walking gingerly downhill with her pacer. As I pass her I can hear her sobbing quietly with the pain of descending on quadricep muscles which are completely shot. Her pacer is silent and so are we - what is there to say? There are still nearly 40 miles to go. I want to reach out to her or something, but the moment passes and I'm not strong enough. We all share a look: 'Hope she makes it...'

But Jamie has a new lease of life and is surging ahead down the narrow trail. Every now and then he catches himself and slows up. Matt runs between us acting as the link in the chain. Jamie is chatting away and I strive to stay animated and keep appreciating the views - but I am going through periods where I simply shut up and get on with the business of putting one foot in front of the other and keeping the boys in sight as they weave along the trail ahead of me. Darkness is falling and I'm having to be increasingly careful where I put my feet: Every trip or stubbed toe sends pain shooting up through my legs. The boys remark on my restraint - which is either a wince or a sharp intake of breath followed by a big exhale. No full-on swearing just yet and I mutter something about the English stiff upper lip...

Night-time. The trail takes a whole new identity through the light of a head-torch, and is marked periodically by glow-sticks hung from trees. It's still warm. I'd been looking forward to this all day - not quite knowing what to expect as the last time I'd played in the woods at night was in my scout days, (!) - and I knew this would be a different, special experience.

The harsh reality is that under torch light it becomes increasingly diffi-cult to read the dips in the trail. This means more stumbles and THAT means more stubbed toes. My already bruised and swollen digits are taking a real hammering, and while we all stumble every now and then, I'm the one who's doing it most.

But I work hard to keep my spirits up and keep talking to the boys. We're still moving pretty well, and the forest is beautiful with stars starting to emerge above the trees. Inside, my pain and frustration mounts with every stumble...

10 miles on and I've discovered the re-vitalising qualities of soup and noodles now being served at the aid stations. If only they'd do tea as well! Every aid station is even more of an oasis now as the bobbing lights thread their way onward.

Matt consults his watch and takes stock.

"We need to make some time up if we're going to do this. We walked too much over that last 10 miles. These next few miles are pretty run-able and we need to run. How you doin', Andy?"

I take a deep breath and prepare a cover story.

"I'm OK. The feet are a bit painful, but everything else is pretty good."

"OK." Matt is all business. "Let's just crack on then and get to the river crossing."

I take the point so it feels like I'm being pushed. I realise that on a clear and flat trail I can make pretty good time - it's just that we don't really have one of those, but this section is good enough! I call the changes back to the boys so they can anticipate in the darkness: "Walk!" when I slow for an uphill. "Dip!" when the trail descends. "Run!" when I'm about to run on again.

But my toes are getting more painful with every stumble - and stumbles are getting more and more frequent. My language is deteriorating and I'm really having to fight the mounting frustration. I simply can't run rocky descents at all now as I'm simply too frightened to trip - so getting my muscles to relax is increasingly difficult. Doing this on top of fatigue from 70 miles of running already just makes it all even more fun! Just give me some easier terrain please!

Despite this, we are making good progress and are not lingering at the interim aid stations. A couple of miles out from the river crossing Matt asks about my weight as we have another check coming up.

"I'm down a little." I reply.

"Well, we don't want to get held at this check," observes Matt, "Are you drinking all your water?"

I hurriedly down a few slurps, "Pretty much..."

"OK. You need to finish that bottle and some more. I've got some spare. And don't pee before the next check. What have you been doing for salts and electrolytes?"

"Er, crisps, fruit, pretzels..."

"Oh, bloody hell!" Matt stops. "No wonder you're struggling! Here, get this down you." He passes over a salt sachet, "That'll do wonders..."

Funnily enough I did seem to perk up...

Going Solo

78 miles. "Great job!" Matt is all smiles. "That's 15 minutes faster than the last section: we're back on schedule! Let's not stop at the aid here - let's get across to the check at the far side."

The river is too swollen for us to wade across as is normal in the race. This year we move with the grace of an arthritic gazelle into a dinghy and are paddled across what is actually a raging torrent in places. Time to part ways, then.

I turn to Jamie. "You go on, mate. I want to grab some food here and I'll follow. If you're still at Green Gate (79m) when I get there, great - if not I'll crack on on my own."

He hesitates. "No, I'll..."

"Bollocks. We said to the river and here we are. It's up to me now, but you need to go if you want to be sure of a 24 hour finish. I'll ****ing get there. If you're still there, great - if not, no worries."

He still temporizes, bless him.

"Well, we'll go ahead and tell Charlotte what's happening so she can be ready and you can be fast through Green Gates..." I smile knowing there's no way I'll be fast through Green Gates: I need to do some serious foot repair work or I'm in real trouble.

I wave him away. "Great - now piss off - GO!"

It's about a mile and a half and a few hundred feet of climbing from the river bank to the next check. Thankfully, after a murderously steep rocky first section, the trail widens, eases and smooths out. I can make good time and arrive around midnight in good spirits not long after Jamie and Matt have left. I can move fast on slight grades and a good surface - anything else... Charly has been here for hours but is delighted to see me as the boys have told her to expect me much later.

Patching Up

"We're going to have to do some running repairs here, babe - scalpel please!" I grin at her and gingerly ease myself down onto the ground trying to multi-task foot duties with slurping noodle soup. We must be making a pretty bad job of it as we're soon interrupted.

"You guys grab this chair - can I help you with anything there?"

Rob is waiting for his wife who is running - we later find out she has sprained both ankles but is still moving! - and has been watching us struggle: We are the only crew without a chair so he has taken pity on us. I ease myself up into a much more comfortable position as Rob ferries food and generally looks after us.

My inspection reveals both big toes are various shades of pink and black and very swollen. It looks like I'll lose both nails as well as a smaller third one on my right foot. There's a hotspot forming at the base of my second toe and first signs of blistering on the outside edge of my right foot. Hmmm...

We clean, pad and strap both feet, re-apply Vaseline and change to new socks. In between I'm chugging down noodle soup by the cupful. It must be quite a scene as a reporter from the LA Times also gets in on the act. All in all it's quite a party! I'm losing time but there's nothing I can do - I need this stop.

Ahead of me is a 15 mile section which I will face on my own with toes that now feel as though they belong to someone else, and quad muscles which are on another planet. This will be the longest and coldest part of the night. However long I think it will take me - and my reckoning is all over the place - add some more and then some.

We're finally done. Big thanks to Rob, a hug and a kiss with Charly - see you at the next big aid station at Highway 49 - and I walk gingerly out. It takes a few attempts to break into a trot but I'm back to my routine of walk-jog-run-trip-swear! The forest folds around me but I'm warmed by the soup and by the fact that I'm moving again. The stars are brilliant above the treetops and despite my halting progress I'm at peace with the world.

6 miles on and I'm still OK and through the 85 mile aid station fortified by chocolate brownies - but then the slide really happens. I'm finding it increasingly difficult to run with any smoothness at all and am stumbling more and more. This just makes it even more painful and however much I try to relax, everything just seems to be tightening up. I can make good speed with a fast walk if the terrain permits - it's just that the terrain is not permitting. Another change: I've stopped passing people and am starting to get passed at will.

Going downhill is a real problem now - and there are still lots of downhills.

Coming Apart

Brown's Bar aid station at 90 miles is one of the most flamboyant on the route. It's Hawaiian themed and decorated with the world's supply of Christmas lights. I can hear rock music blasting out down the valley from miles away! I arrive with a couple of other folks and we can't help but smile at the sensory overload which greets us. The spirit of the volunteers would cheer the dead - and that's pretty close to what they're doing!

I go for the chocolate brownies and noodle soup again.

"How far to the next check?'"

"3 miles."

3 miles. I can do that.

But a few yards beyond the aid station it looks like it could all end. Facing another steep rocky descent through the torchlight I find my legs simply won't work and I come to a juddering halt. For a while I simply stand there baffled. OK. Maybe if I'm warmer I'll be able to do it. So I put on every piece of clothing that I'm carrying and try again.

It's pathetic: I can't make my legs go where I want them at all. This is ****ing unbelievable - COME ON!

I stumble haltingly down but the breaking point comes at a rocky stream crossing. Stepping across using the various rocks seems be-

76

yond me, and it simply doesn't occur to me to get my feet wet. I'm reduced to tears of frustration as a number of tentative steps get me absolutely nowhere. Eventually summoning the motor skill reserves to place my feet where I want them is a massive effort - and I'm emotionally and physically wrung out when I reach the other side.

JESUS CHRIST!

I'm doing pathetic lurching now, and it seems that people are streaming past. Even short climbs reduce me to moving in slow motion because I can't seem to get my left hip to work now to lift my knee. I've heard of Keeping It Simple - just keep moving forward! - but this is ridiculous and it's all taking too long: Far too long.

My thoughts are turning increasingly to Charly. I remember our wedding and a whole montage of shared highlights. I remember how tough this waiting is for her - and what a long day she has had already. I remember that out here I'm representing us both - and you're doing a pretty poor ****ing job of it right now, sunshine!

Yeah, if it matters, it hurts to fall short...

I desperately want to do this in a way we can both be proud of - and that never included stumbling about like a direction-less idiot in the small hours. Everything else feels fine - it just my bloody legs!!!

It's taking way too long. She's waiting and wondering...IT'S JUST NOT ****ING FAIR!

I spend the next few miles trying control the emotional roller coaster of love for my lady and the pain and frustration of what I'm reduced to. The final climb to the aid station nearly finishes me: I'm moving SO slowly and literally dragging my left leg up and there's seems absolutely nothing I can do about it. I just want to burst into tears but manage to bite it down every time.

Part of me is dreading seeing her at Highway 49.

Dead right. I walk miserably into the aid station, on and off the weighing scales without seeing or caring, and promptly burst into tears on my wife's shoulder.

I'm absolutely distraught and cry my eyes out telling her that I love her, that I'm sorry she's had to wait so long, that I just can't go any faster, that everything else is fine, that she's the best thing that's ever happened to me...it just pours out. Charly sits there holding me going all misty-eyed while dawn breaks around us and our American audience has some preconceptions busted about stiff upper-lip Brits...

And then it all stops. I dry my eyes, drink some soup, shed my night gear, smile, kiss her, and get up and walk unsteadily on.

7 miles to go. Well, it would be rude not to, wouldn't it?

Mending & Ending

I'm joined in this last section by Hawaii-Matt. Matt had been pacing someone earlier who had dropped out at 75m. Feeling redundant and seeing an obvious need, (!) he offered to keep me company. I was glad of it, and though the first few miles I was very quiet, conversation picked up as we made our way very slowly to the finish.

Charly came out and joined us for the final mile as we walked in slow motion through the outskirts of Auburn. Locals in their gardens cheering and 'high-fiving' us as we passed. They've painted Tour De France style on the roads. Wow. Smile, man - you're nearly there now.

An honoury 3/4 lap of the high school track - no, I'm still not running, thanks - and finally, eventually, 27 hours and 15 minutes later, it's over.

100 miles

21,970 feet of descent

18, 040 feet of ascent

One day - and a little bit extra

A few tears

Lots of smiles

Some sore feet and lifelong friends

And a little bit of heart and soul.

It's really nice to be here...

I'm walking, it's slow, but I'm in and that will do.

2007

We moved house - finally - from Leicestershire to North Yorkshire. It took us over a year - with all the usual nightmares that seem to be a normal part of buying and selling houses in England - but finally we got there. First baby (Tom) arrived in April, we had a death in the family around the same time - and four months later we moved. Then spent the rest of the year figuring out how to do this parenting thing...

I kept a separate diary during Charlotte's pregnancy and one of the things I'm shocked by when reading it again, was how much time and energy I seemed to spend doing anger. Anger at the frustration of the house move, anger at the fight we went through to get support for a home birth, anger at the difficulties of running my own business, anger at the apparent untimeliness of the death of my granddad. Of course, it's all completely self-directed as us blokes are hard-wired to fix things and provide all the answers without ever once asking for help...I mean, there was unbridled joy as well (!) but, man, I had some issues!

Running? Five races which included my second outing over a six day stage race format in Andalucia, Spain. All of them nothing to write home about in performance terms. My diary is packed with work-move-baby stuff AND I'm still travelling lots AND still training hard with plenty of biking to complement the running. Something had to give and something did. I took an injury and infection out to Marathon of Spain and came back with worse.

Marathon of Spain came three months after Tom arrived and there was much soul searching and debate between Mr & Mrs Mouncey about the rights and wrongs of going. In the end we figured it would be good therapy for Daddy. And while I came back injured I also had a very moving flow experience, met some lovely people, travelled through some amazing landscape and got a few things in perspective.

Marathon of Spain 2007: Finding The Flow

Six Day Stage Race, Andalucia

"Sometimes you're just at peace with the world, y'know?"

And with that I smile to the crew, shoulder my pack, douse water over my head and arms one final time, and jog off into the searing heat once again - except this time I'm smiling very happily and almost whistling!

A great shot of what it was like: Hot, dusty and rocky.

It's about 11 km to checkpoint five and big wide trail the whole way.

I'm quickly into my running and am smiling at how dramatic the mood shift has been: after getting a real kicking on the last quarter of the 3000 feet straight-up climb we've just navigated between checkpoint 3-4: I'm now one very happy little camper.

Despite passing through one of the most physically intimidating landscapes I've ever been in, I'm completely at one with myself and the world around me.

The surrounding mountainscape is an immense 360 degree perspective, the trail ahead unrelenting rocky track, the temperature nudging 43 degrees Centigrade, and the huge flat-bottomed valley I am travelling along makes me feel like a grain of sand against it all...Yeah, you don't figure much out here, my friend...

The brutal climb had forced me to lose contact with Jacques and Dan, with whom I have run for the first 25 miles today. A combination of searing heat, cumulative effort, and gradient which nearly had me on hands and knees, saw me grind to a halt some three quarters of the way into this two hour bitch of a climb during the hottest part of the day. With my breathing threatening to spiral out of control and my heart feeling as though it was about to burst through my chest, I was forced to stop in the shade of a nearby tree.

'You're OK, man - just breathe, sit up, be calm, and breathe. Take some water and stay with it - it'll pass...stay with it...'

I remember the complete spiral out of control at the top of yesterday's climb with about 10km to go. We'd deliberately run hard for the first 2.5 hours to try and cover as much ground before the temperature hit the 40's. It was a day with absolutely no shade on the entire route - which meant that we were to be steadily cooked at the sun's leisure...

Out of the red and into the shade. Gathering myself for the last part of the stage.

Three days into the race I now knew that I could balance the variables on a big climb to give me forward progress: how hot it was, how steep and long the hill, my cadence and posture - and finally the level of effort and the rate of breathing. Trying to keep up with anyone else - racing - was a shortcut to disaster: I'd tried this yesterday and the result had me flat on my back at the top of the climb willing my heart and lungs back inside my shuddering body.

(That I later learned that Fulvio, our Italian veteran and winner of Stage 1, was throwing up and Dan was bleeding through his nose on the very same climb was no consolation: *Focus On What You Can Control*, man...)

One day later and this time it's different: I'm still looking into the abyss - but this time I'm only admiring the view.

'Stay with this, man - give it time, it'll come back to you...c'mon, you've got this...'

Jacques and Dan climb away into the distance, but meanwhile in the shady layby of sorts equilibrium is returning.

The boys are now out of sight and out of mind. Dan is clearly having a great day while Jacques continues to float his way over the mountains. Behind me by about half an hour is the only other person left in the race and on the course. The only lady to start the race, Jo Kilkenny set off this morning an hour ahead of us determined to do her thing on this longest of stages. We had passed her and her mountain bike escort Mark at checkpoint three looking like she'd not a care in the world. She'll do just fine today...

Except I really am not alone out here. With me are my wife Charlotte and our new baby son Tom. Over the next few kilometres the three of us run easily through the furnace: Sometimes we are chatting away, sometimes we just touch each other with our smiles. It doesn't matter that no-one else can see them... and maybe it's not quite such a coincidence that now, finally, after three days of being stripped raw, on Day Four of this race, I feel whole again.

I know that I'll finish the stage and that I'll do it in my own time and my own way.

It doesn't matter to me how fast, and it doesn't matter to me by when.

Right now? I'm just enjoying being...

Here's something that preparing to swim the English Channel in 2003 taught me about *flow*. And I think that when we are talking about performance we are talking about how to attain this flow state - this line of least resistance.

Acceptance comes first - total and absolute. Acceptance of the environment and of everything and anything it may throw at you: it's the wallpaper - you can't change it and you can't ignore it - so roll with it. Welcome everything.

Acceptance also of you: who you are, what you stand for and what baggage you bring. In this place there is no hiding - indeed, there is no need to hide, because acceptance of the whole can be a path to contentment in the present. Relax - enjoy the journey!

Respect comes next: respect for a huge physical environment - and there's nothing like ocean swimming and mountain running to make you feel insignificant - such that it feels like you almost ask permission to pass safely through just this one time...no trace, no litter, no noise... just my wake or my footprints, and the sea or the wind will soon wipe those away as well.

Then there's Trust and Belief. Trust the environment to keep you safe. Belief that you possess everything you need to do whatever it is you need to do right now and over these next few hours. Belief that right now, you are in exactly the right place doing exactly the right thing, in exactly the right way.

...feel how you need to feel in order to do what it is you want to do...

Yeah. Performance Is Emotional all right...and right now for me out here, the dial is turned all the way up to No 11...

And if that lot doesn't make you smile...

What a difference to the first three days out here.

Patrick, Jacque, Fulvio, Me, Dan at the start of day 4

2008

Our first full year in our new home in North Yorkshire as Tom grows up and becomes a toddler. Eight months into parenthood at the start of the year and we are still wrestling with it and each other. My diary records at least some of the ups and downs that are magnified as the business ebbs and flows as credit crunch hits. 'Rocky' would be a good description!

15 races in the buildup to the first Lakeland 100 - which will be only my second outing over the distance. I get a personal best at the 24 mile Three Peaks fellrace in April, and my ass kicked by my pairs partner Alex in my first mountain marathon (LAMM) in Scotland early June. And don't ask me about the midgies...

My prep for L100 is all-around course familiarity and I cover some sections five times before I'm happy. My logic is that it simply means I have more energy for the task of moving forward relentlessly if I know where I'm going...

That part really works, but comparing this first year with 2011 and I'm astonished by some of the differences in my beliefs and preparation.

Then for the rest of the year there are just huge blanks in my diary with periodic paragraphs of detail. I'm putting some quality benchmark sessions in around some high intensity conditioning work, and while skin infections come and go (immune system a bit compromised then) I am injury-free for much of the year. Some programmed recovery time would have been welcome because by November I'd pretty much fizzled out.

Lakeland 100 2008: Rubbed Up Raw

Up close and very personal in the inaugural running of the Ultra Tour Of The Lake District

100 miles - Two Feet - One Day

Running Repairs

'I bet those **!!** sheep must be getting seriously worried!'

The only reason I can't lift my head to check is that I am concentrating hard on the Task At Hand which is this:

I'm at 65 miles on an exposed open fellside climbing to the high point of the entire route. It's torrential rain, howling wind and I'm wearing nothing below my waist except for my running shoes.

So I know what you're thinking - and it's not that

It's this:

You see, ultra-marathon running is a contact sport and that contact comes in three parts. There's feet-to-ground, (that's the obvious one) then there's rucksack or bumbag to shoulders or waist, and then for the fellas there's there real killer: chafing to the undercarriage.

I'm guessing this passes the ladies by, but you're right: I've never actually asked...

Despite liberal coatings of vaseline it's all been getting steadily worse over the last 15 miles or so to the point where I'm about to start crying like a girl.

Really.

And that would never do.

Fortunately in desperate times the old grey matter can come up with desperate measures, and mine has done just that.

I grit my teeth for what I hope will be the last time to gingerly apply more lube to the offending area while the wind tries its best to ram the raindrops through my cheeks and then hurl me off the slope: '****!!'

Then I spend frantic minutes wrestling my overtrousers back over my shoes and up my legs. Strap kit back on and tie down. Stand and test: 'Oh yes! YES!!'

A wave of what I can describe as almost sexual relief washes through me - if I had a cigarette right now I'd reach for it.

I'll run the next 20 miles or so commando-style but so what: I'm back to chafe-free running, and let me tell you, it feels goooood!

It's A Monster. With Very Big Teeth

Some 15 hours or so earlier at 7.30pm on Friday August 8th some 30 hardy souls had set off from Coniston with 100 miles and some 19,000 feet of climbing and descending in front of them and a 40 hour schedule to beat as the first Ultra Tour Of The Lake District (UTLD) got underway.

Look at all the people! 33 very nervous runners lining up (sort of) for the first Lakeland 100

Modelled on the Ultra Tour Of Mont Blanc on the continent which now attracts some 2000 athletes and fills up within hours of the entries going live on-line, NW-based adventure racer and endurance athlete Marc Laithwaite had decided that anything the French could do...so he and his team had come up with a clockwise loop through the Lake District that would prove to be a monster. With very big teeth.

Welcome To Our World

Now people don't generally get on the start line of a 100 miler unless they're ready, so the finish rates are normally pretty high.

Not this time.

Less than half the field would finish this first race - the rest would be either timed out at checkpoints or would retire with a few stories to tell.

There are a handful of factors which make 100 milers such an undertaking:

- The cumulative mileage which drains body and brain
- The night section(s) which demand concentration
- The navigation - made harder by 1,2,4, & 6
- The isolation which can be as intimidating as the distance
- The amount of (rough) descending which trashes the legs
- The weather
- The need to stay awake and keep your wits about you

Any one of these can be the difference between a finish and a DNF.

All seven together? Welcome to the world of the UTLD!

Playing Smart

I walk the first mile or so at the back of the field which is tough 'cos I'm ready for this and I wanna play with the boys at the front. But this is a deliberate decision made for three reasons:

1. It will mean that I'll run at my pace when I get going.
2. I'll always be moving past people which always feels good!
3. I won't be giving anyone a free ride with the navigation.

It's this final one which is the biggie: I've recced the entire route including the night section at night, and I reckon very few other folks - if any - will have done the same. So I know I know where I'm going - and I want to keep it that way for as long as possible…

We head SW then curve round north to the first checkpoint at Seath-waite. I'm reckoning on doing the first 20-25 miles on momentum and am focusing on 'floating' my way through the field expending the least amount of energy possible. Crazy as it may sound, I do regard this as the 'freebie.' I also know we'll get this first stage done before darkness after which my world reduces down to a headtorch beam for about seven hours.

I catch a group of six lying third just before the checkpoint and hang back so they hit the checkpoint first. I know there are some navigation choices to be made just the other side of the checkpoint, so my mind is clear: I'm straight in, fill my doggy bag and straight out again and off down the road ahead of them.

Keeping my headtorch off in the gathering gloom I work to get out of sight through the woods. No chance! Voices and torchlight behind me signal we are back together again, so I pull over and let the boys go ahead. Oh well! I walk and eat as we climb out north of Seathwaite and console myself with the knowledge that there are plenty more chances to come...But I do love these little games!

Working Through

And sure enough a few miles later we are all reunited as we trudge and trip through the sodden and rock and root-strewn path which winds its way through the forest at the base of Harter Fell. I was here for my final scouting trip on this section only five days ago so I know the dark wet pools are not actually that deep and where the firmest footing is. Time to go! A brief exchange of greetings and I splash ahead.

I know there is a tricky rocky descent coming up again with navigation choices and while my torch will be visible I'm banking on the fact that I'll be moving more confidently and faster over steep loose wet rock. I check the markers off in my head: over the stile, head to cross the stream through the gap in the wall...now where's the line between the two rocky outcrops? OK, through and drop down - CAREFUL! - then hard left at the post over the wet bit and head to parallel the wall... WATCH IT! It's ankle-wrenching stuff here - you're supposed to be floating, remember?!

But it is working and I move steadily ahead, gaining confidence as I pass the familiar markers in this first tricky night section. Next stop checkpoint two at Boot.

The welcome and warmth of the pub is very tempting, but I'm not stopping for last orders. A swift cup of soup, grab some sandwiches to go, and I'm out, keeping my torch off again till I'm out of sight of the group I know are only a few minutes behind.

I munch my way through the village passing late night pub-goers. 'You're third!' shouts a voice through the darkness. Third? Let's go find second, then...

Phone A Friend?

We're now making a beeline for Wasdale which I'm reckoning to be about an hour away. This is the second tricky navigation bit because as we climb clear of Boot the landscape becomes increasingly featureless with multiple path choices - all kinda ending up where we want to be, but only one taking the direct route. I've concluded that the only way to be sure to get the right path junction in the pitch black is to count paces from the final gate - I'm not wearing a watch so timing it is pointless - but the required 700 paces later I'm still not at the junction. That was 700 - wasn't it? But it clearly wasn't 'cos I don't recognise the ground: 'Should be another flat, wet rocky bit and then it kicks up again...'

I jog on, sweeping my light to the right searching for the marker stone I placed on the tiny cairn. Where is that rocky bit? I know I've not passed it...

Then out of the darkness I recognise the puddles, the path kicks up and then there's my marker stone - gotcha! This is the first of the two keys to the stage - but I'm stuffed if I've lost my ability to count already!

Lights ahead - two of them. I'm closing fast which I can only assume means that they're lost or unsure. I'm neither and say a silent prayer of thanks again that I've done my homework. This stage will really mess with you if you get it wrong.

A fresh breeze from my left announces our arrival at Burnmoor Tarn and the three of us coincide for the first time. I don't know it yet but Warren and Nick are a couple of seasoned adventure racers up from London (Nick Gracie as a world champion being no slouch at all) and I remember them being conspicuous at the start clutching their poles. (I'd reckoned it's just more kit to lug around - an opinion I will revise on reflection post-race...)

Brief greetings and some gallows humour about time and place, then I'm off, concentrating hard on getting the right line off the NE edge which is the second key to this stage.

Hug the shore - you know it's all flooded here - and watch for the track rising slightly still on the same line. Got it! Grass for a couple of hundred yards then fork sharp right at the base of a short steep climb. I grin as I remember this is where Alex and I practically tripped over a cow lying right across the path on our night recce. Well, you expect sheep on the fells, don't you? But something four times the size looming into the torchlight is another thing entirely!

I can hear the other two are tagging on behind and smile ruefully. I've reconciled myself up front on the 'drop or stick' choices. I know there are either specific locations where route choices have to be made, or where if I go hard, I can get out of sight of any chasers. But this is not where I am right now, and you can't exactly zip away over rocky, wet, uneven ground in the pitch black anyway.

Well, you could if you were Jos Naylor, and we are heading into the great man's backyard...

I know that if Nick and Warren decide I am running decisively - i.e it looks like I know where I'm going - odds are they'll tag me: I know I would!

The 64 thousand dollar question: Am I prepared to expend energy to deliberately drop them, or do I conserve and see how the elastic expands or contracts between us as we go?

Phone a friend??

In The Slipstream Of Steve

We slither down into Wasdale Head together, in and out the check-point sharpish, and set our sights on Lake Buttermere to the north. Our route will take us over the first two of the high passes: Black Sail and Scarth Gap before dropping down to the lake. I grin when I remember that it took my wife Charlotte as long to drive between these two checkpoints as it did for me to run this stage - which I chose to interpret as my speedy running as opposed to her limited road choices!

We will have two big, steep, rocky, wet descents to negotiate on this leg - and I came a right cropper on the second one during my night recce. Let's keep the runner on the feet this time, please!

I find Wasdale Head such an atmospheric place. Hemmed in on three sides by steep mountains, I hoped I would see it with a clear starlit sky. No chance! The clouds have thrown a blanket over everything though the cloud base is above our high point.

Up and down the first climb with no worries and just the sound of water rushing down the mountainside around us. Torch light is glimpsed behind us as we switchback - but it is a long way down. But my focus is on the way ahead. Eyes front, sunshine!

Smoothly up and over the second smaller climb, and safely down the long descent to the western shore of Buttermere. Then at the checkpoint in the village we get the first news of the leader: "Steve is 50 minutes ahead of you." I figure I've misheard. "You mean 15 - one, five don't you?"

Er, no.

Steve Birkinshaw has flown off the front and coming up to a third of the way round is indeed 50 minutes up. Bloody hell! We've haven't exactly been dawdling, but then I remember that if he did fly off the front from the start he probably gained half that time on me on the first stage. Well, fair play to the fella: if he comes back he comes back - now let's get back to focusing on what you can control, man...

Breaking Free

We're still heading north and this next leg will see us in sight of Keswick and hopefully into sunrise! Before that, we have to thread our way on narrow, faint climbing paths. It looked straightforward on the map My recces have shown me it is anything but, and the potential for disaster is huge.

So it's an ideal stage to play my advantage, but to do that would have meant getting out of the checkpoint ahead of Warren and Nick and going hard to get out of sight. And I've lost that chance. If I let them go ahead I'll catch them and even if I get past they'll have my torchlight to follow.

So I really made my choice coming along the lake shore.

I smile ruefully as I go through an inventory - then admit that at least part of me will be glad of the company on this final dark stage.

It's a perfect stage navigation-wise and we are even blessed with a clearing sky part way through. We all stop and stare up into the starscape: 'One of the reasons we do this, man...

We hit the checkpoint at Braithwaite on the outskirts of Keswick still chasing the dawn - still no sign of the sky lightening. Bowls of rice pudding and pasta devoured in quick succession then we gird our loins for some road bashing into Keswick.

It's here that our elastic snaps for the first time. A call of nature delays me, the boys miss a turn ahead of me, I dive down it and come out ahead.

Clear for the first time for hours, I put my head down and work to put some time on them as we climb back onto the fells northeast of Keswick.

It's fine balance between effort and control but I keep my eyes firmly ahead and my attention of the controls. Once the forest above Keswick has been left behind, this whole section is open. Even if I'm a considerable distance ahead I know the boys will be able to see me on the dogleg across the valley. So I work on the principle practised by small children the world over: If I can't see you, you can't see me!

Warning Lights

Blencathra Centre is the last checkpoint before Dockray - and Dockray is half way.

The marshals emerge cold and windswept from the shelter of a wall. It's not exactly city station out here! I am now lying second - and I'm told Steve has increased his lead again, on schedule for a 12 hour first half.

This means that I am 'late' - but I don't figure this till I look at the timings after the race as I have set no schedules, I don't have a watch, and I'm not interested in the time. Right there, all I know is that:

I need to keep eating and drinking

The tough night stuff is behind us

And I still have my proverbial **** together

I'm only gone a couple of miles into the next stage when I hear a shouted greeting behind me. No prizes: Warren and Nick are a couple of hundred yards away.

Okayyyyyy - so much for that whopping great gap you thought you opened up then!

We finally come together for the last four miles into the checkpoint, and by then we are all focused on the fact that we are in touching distance of half way:

- It's stayed dry
- We all have new kit and food to look forward to
- My feet are still in one piece
- And I still have my **** together

But I know I have a problem developing, because among the green dials there is one starting to flash amber. I've been on mainly solid food for the first few hours, and much of it has gone through me which has necessitated multiple emergency dumping action.

I've since switched to gels but it would appear the damage is done...

My shorts have also been starting to chafe - I've tested this short/pants combo over seven hours so clearly it's good for that and no extra(!) - and worryingly, no amount to vaseline seems to help. It's not an area you really want to have problems with when you are on your Jack Jones in the middle of a mountainside with miles left to go. Yeah, if you're gonna have a sense of humour failure over anything, sunshine, this one will do it in spades...

Put simply I have one priority: at halfway I really need to sort my **** out.

Rubbing Up The Wrong Way

Sometimes stuff has to get worse before it gets better: The weather deteriorated to the wind and rain we would get for the rest of the day, (and night) and my next 15 miles were dominated by increasing discomfort, deceasing vaseline supplies, and increasing number and duration of emergency stops to administer to my tenderizing undercarriage.

In between all this I was still running strongly - I'd just get to a point where I'd have to stop, make an adjustment, and scream at something for a bit - so once again Nick, Warren and I were all leapfrogging each other - a pattern we kept till the last quarter or so of the race.

Then at Pooley Bridge just short of 60 miles there's my wife with our baby son Tom who wastes no time in practising his own brand of waving to his grinning daddy. They've been here since Steve blew through - hours ago - because that was our Plan A as well...

Smiles and cold kisses all round: 'Hi honey - be with you in a minute - just need to dive into these public toilets..!' I'm such a romantic.

Full Circle

Salvation awaits me at Ambleside. Not only are Tom and Charlotte waiting, but the checkpoint is in the Lakes Runner shop - and as far as I am concerned, shop only means one thing: New shorts!

I am weary and I'm sore and I've been getting progressively slower on the climbs. I just can't move my legs any faster! It's also been dreadful weather since breakfast time - but you know what else? I'm a little over 80 miles to the good and I do still have my wits about me. I know that I just need to sort myself out, smile with my favourite lady and our new small boy and we'll be in business for the last bit.

"Have you still got your headtorch, Andy?"

Huh?

"You'll need a light, babe - it'll be dark before you finish now."

I'm momentarily confused as I'd never considered the prospect that I'd be finishing in the dark, but Charly is right - and I ditched my torch at 50 miles.

Thank god we're in a shop then!

I'm off and moving again as the town is closing up for the day.

Darkness does finally set in for the second time when I am at about six miles to go. Well before that I have decided that I will walk it in when that happens because it is more important for me to:

- Finish
- Finish safely
- Finish without putting myself into a bigger box than I am already inhabiting...

But it is a very slow walk. It's still raining and the tracks are now mainly raging torrents. The last few miles are at high level in the pitch black with the mist reducing visibility down to 20 yard torch beam while Mother Nature does her thing with a thunderstorm in the near distance.

This is a sting in the tail and no mistake!

But I'm a happy camper even though my world has shrunk down to the bare essentials.

Very close now...

I'm tortoise slow down the final big steep rocky treacherous descent, remembering how I danced down this in training - and then all that is left is the walk back down the track we started out on.

I get lost trying to find my way through a short cut in Coniston - and I can practically see the finish, for god's sake!!! - but eventually at some point just before midnight I am walking up the drive to the Sports Club towards a very familiar silhouette.

"Hi honey." A big long hug. 'It's very nice to be back."

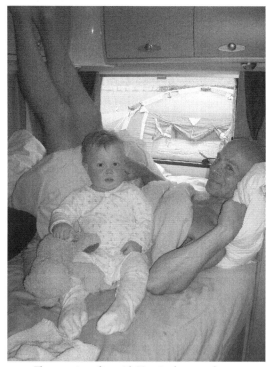

The morning after with Tom in the motorhome

2009-2010

An 'all over the place' year and the running reflects that. Everything happens in context, right? A credit crunch has meant that the bottom had dropped out of my corporate training work towards the end of last year - and I'd had most of my eggs in that basket - so this was the first year of real struggle. On top of that we were practising the skills of parenting our first toddler who was not really sleeping...My diary records many sleepless interrupted nights, bouts of doing depression interspersed with almost manic direction-less activity as I cast about for the magic pill for Daddy-Husband-Businessman-Runner. Huge highs and plunging lows and not much in between.

Six races all year and they all come before mid March.

At the end of April we get the fantastic news that Charly is pregnant for the second time - huge huge high!

Sometime in June we stare into the financial abyss with £££ fast disappearing and no work (and new baby) on the horizon.

I start training in May in earnest for a second crack at L100 and eight weeks later I am in superb shape and the lightest I've been for a long time. My diary records a floating 9.5 hours solo on the Dalesway long distance footpath, and an equally effortless eight hour solo night recce on the L100 route in the western fells. Those are the highlights.

Then breakdown follows swiftly: I've been experimenting with barefoot/minimal running, no stretching and have changed my running style. Shorter steps and more on the fore/mid-foot means I feel much lighter and more efficient, but my lower legs are not up to the rate of progression I'm asking. I take it to the point of complete failure - I can barely walk - and as a serious infection sets in around my eyes just for good measure I finally get the message: immune system trashed and lower legs musculature totally shot. Thank you and goodnight. There is to be no return to the L100 this year.

Huge blanks in the diary till October - though I had started to swim(?!) and bike again slowly in September - then gradually some routine returns.

Joe is born nearly three weeks 'late' amidst huge snows at home two days before Christmas.

In 2010 something new and some unfinished business - but it took a wee while to get going. Another tough year business-wise and my diary records periodic bouts of 'doing depression', illness and big blanks on the pages Jan - May where I just refused to come out of my cave. We had a new baby in the family - something that brought great joy and equally great adjustment, and Daddy was still finding it hard to put bread on the table.

So Fellsman early May, (Something New) was a bit of therapy. I'd had my head kicked in at the 24 mile Three Peaks Fellrace a couple of weeks earlier and I recall going into this one as 'sod it - head up, enjoy, and let's see what happens...'

Unfinished Business was back at my old friend L100, and after missing last year I'd put together 10 good weeks of prep - only to badly roll my ankle and sprain ligaments 10 days before the race. I knew I was in good shape, but would my strategy mean I fly or fall?

Then out to France to work for a week coaching on Alpine Oasis Trail Running Camps before spectating at Ultra Tour Mont Blanc - WOW!!

13 races before Lakeland at the end of July and then nothing for the rest of the year - just training: An average of 7.5 hours a week mix of bike-run-conditioning from September to Christmas. My diary also records a hefty dose of quality sessions as the norm with lotsa benchmark sessions recording progressive (or regressive) times.

Fellsman 2010: Finding Form

May 8, 2010: 62 miles / 11,200'

It's not a good start.

Halfway up Whernside the second mountain of the day - there are nine - I'm sitting on my backside with both shoes and socks off surrounded by bits of my first aid kit while concentrating firmly on the task of taping my heels.

And I'd been worried enough, thank you, without this little addition.

I mean, you would be too, right, contemplating 62 miles of up hill and down Yorkshire dale on the back of little and sporadic specific training when the last race you did two weeks previously over a pathetic 24 miles had you hanging on like a dying dog over the final third?

Still, sometimes the only way to really see where you're at is to really see where you're at.

So I'd swallowed hard and made some mental adjustments.

Chief among these was to push Competitive Running Bloke right down into the bottom of my rucksack: today would not be about him.

Today would be about head up, enjoy the views and the company, relax and keep everything in the green. Get to know the route for next time - so there'll be a next time? - and finish with plenty still in the tank.

Got that?

My pre-start activity did set the tone: chasing our very excited three year old round the start area. He's intent on demonstrating his capacity for interval training with simultaneous commentary all at high volume: "Look at me, Daddy! I'm a really fast runner!"

This meant I chugged off quite happily way down the field of over 400 souls with a smile on my face mentally ticking off the 'happy box'.

Thanks, son.

Warming up with Tom

This continued up the first climb of Ingleborough as I threaded my way through the field pausing now and then to chat to folks I recognised and some I didn't.

The hotspots on both heels started on the approach to Whernside, and while I am wearing brand new trainers this is not unusual for me: I'd used the same make, model and size straight out of the box for years with no problems.

Except today.

Today there will be screaming and crying and gnashing of teeth and rending of clothes later if I don't STOP RIGHT NOW and sort this out.

So I press 'eject' on the lovely, calm, happy world with gorgeous views and easy running I'd been enjoying and get decisive about Reality.

Right, over this next stile then...

Rucksack off, sit down, shoes and socks off.

Footcare kit out, examine the damage. Yep, blisters about the size of 50p starting on the backs of both heels, but no fluid build-up yet and it looks clean.

Good. Tape and strap. Make sure to get a good seal.

On with the shoes and socks taking care to lace firmly - I suspect that was the problem: sloppy, Andy, very sloppy - repack the sack, stand and test.

It's as fast as I can make it, but Competitive Running Bloke escapes and whispers that many minutes and lots of people have gone past.

I push him back down: Today is not your day...

Now, where were we?

Whernside is the first chance to get a look at the leaders as there's an out and back detour to the summit. Steve Birkinshaw thunders past looking like he's doing six miles not 60, followed by Mr Fellsman himself 11-time winner Mark Hartell and a bunch of other faces I recognise.

I have a little smile to myself and chug on upwards as the wind does its best to blow us all off the ridge, but the view really is to die for.

It takes me to Dent (about one third distance) to catch up with Pete again whom I'd run with as we'd come off Ingleborough. It's windy on the tops, sure, but the sun is out periodically and lack of recent rain has given lovely underfoot conditions. I'm running easy, climbing strongly and being Polite Sociable Chappie at checkpoints.

Dent village is the first big food stop.

I refuel to strict nutritional guidelines all at the cutting edge of endurance sport: sausage roll (warm) and cheese sandwich washed down with a mug of tea.

(Well, this race is staged by Keighley Scouts and when in Rome...)

SE on the long climb out of Dent on the Craven Way talking 'stuff' with Pete as we head to the next top of Blea Moor. This is the first real route choice piece across open ground which is a key feature of the second half of the Hike route. Decisions are therefore a combination of your own navigation certainty, local knowledge, and the lines any other runner is taking in front of - or immediately behind you.

Sure, it's so much easier to follow...as long as you're cool with ceding control, (and all the implications in that) and comfortable with doing the freeloading bit.

We nail it and head into the checkpoint at Stone House for another big feed and a moment of levity:

"Secret kit check, lads!"

We're pounced on by a group of Scouts armed with clipboards and armfuls of enthusiasm.

Secret kit check?

"Yeah, everyone's getting it!"

So, erm, it's not much of a secret then, is it?

Guess you had to be there...

The big climb up Great Knoutberry is the final one before halfway and also a second chance to check people in front on the out and back to the summit.

Competitive Running Bloke clocks the faces, notes the gaps and presents his report.

I grunt and file it away under 'No Further Action'.

Halfway and Pete and I are drinking tea in the big checkpoint tent on the road between Hawes to the north and Ingleton to the south. I know we've been on the go for over six hours but I've no idea how much more. Closer to 7? Well, I'm not wearing a watch and I'm really not that interested. Am I?

Of much more interest are the faces and postures of runners in the tent, the refreshments on offer, and the realisation that I'm still feeling Mr Perky.

Must be his lucky day.

Pete and I have been 'biggin' each other up' (as young and cool people say these days) periodically over the last section which has helped keep the momentum going. He is however, vaguely disgusted at my seeming ability to put away solid food at a rapid rate - he complains his digestive juices have gone walkabout and his mastication capacity seems somewhat diminished. Well, there's always those lovely gels...

And so the fun begins.

The second half of the race is full of difficult going over open ground where navigation, route choice, and an ability to move efficiently over the rough stuff will pretty much dictate whether you are Fun To Be With - or not.

And while Pete and I make good time on the approach to Dodd Fell, we lose it all on the final climb to the top and the descent line. It's all grass tussocks, heather, and dry peat bogs - and you either know where to find the sheep trogs and quad bike tracks, or you don't.

We fall into the latter category, though still arrive at Fleet Moss in time to clock the Usual Suspects either in or just leaving the checkpoint. So, not lost that much then...or you lot are hanging about a bit here.

It is tempting.

I have reckoned getting across Fleet Moss with sanity intact is the crux of the whole route, and while it is unseasonably dry, the whole area is a mass of intricate up down peat bog beds that just sap the will and the legs.

The route choice is to either just go for it straight across on a bearing or to take a longer and more runnable route round the southern edge - though this second option only opens up if you know it's there in the first place. Once again, route knowledge is a huge advantage, and care with your nav absolutely essential.

I seriously consider getting straight through the checkpoint in order to hook up with one of the runners ahead of us who is just leaving and I know he knows the route. And while I've also done my homework, I'm looking for some additional security on the section that has concerned me most. It also means I jump a bunch of places and make a chunk of time, because I'm also clocking that many of these guys are starting to hang around longer at checkpoints.

And are sitting down.

Yep, Competitive Running Bloke makes a massive full frontal appearance and I am hugely, hugely tempted...but only briefly.

Today is not that day.

Time to change channels.

Relax, feed, chat, feel good about progress and register a familiar face slumped in a corner. Charlie, bless him, looks on his chinstrap and as about as enthusiastic about this next bit as, well...

Time for a pick-up, then.

We go south with Charlie tagging and a handful of runners strung out in front of us which we periodically catch sight of as the ground opens up. It's compass-contour stuff over stop-start terrain and a relief to finally catch sight of the summit trig on the high point of Middle Tongue.

Two smiling faces emerge from the checkpoint tent on the wind-blasted summit in the middle of nowhere - the things some people do for fun - and then we're off on the final leg-sapping tricky section. Charlie has rallied big-style as we all stumble-jog-walk towards enticingly-named Hell Gap. A final piece of easy running on a good track brings us to Cray at the foot of the penultimate climb up Buckden Pike.

It's now pretty much south to the finish and in my mind we're on the last section. I'm still Mr Chipper, Pete's chugging along happily, and Charlie is a completely different bloke from the one who scraped himself off the floor at Fleet Moss. We put Buckden Pike behind us and not long after find ourselves being grouped for safety at the checkpoint at the foot of the final climb up Great Whernside. We're now a group of seven and will run together as darkness falls sometime after 9pm.

And that's pretty much it.

There's no drama, the head-torches come out for about the final hour, and sometime around 10.30pm I find myself ambling down the final road descent into Grassington and the finish feeling like I've just been round the block.

I've slowed so I can enjoy the quiet on my own, watch the stars come out, and wonder at a day that has allowed me to move beyond all my fears and worries.

So it's just running, is it?

Yeah, right.

The Lakeland 100 2010: Finished Business

It's A Taper, Jim - But Not As You Know It

"Well, Mr Mouncey, the good news is that it's not broken."

My entire being deflates about three sizes as every orifice that can exhales air.

Except I already know the bad news.

With 10 days to go to the start of the L100 I am sitting in a wheel chair outside the X-ray department of Kendal A & E wearing a grimace and a right ankle the size of a small football courtesy of badly sprained ligaments.

I've been out on my final big training run on the western part of the course when my foot just rolled from under me while coming off a rocky descent to send me crashing.

I lay there stunned for a few seconds before the pain came - convinced something was broken.

I was in the middle of nowhere and the only way I was getting back to my car was through my own efforts. So with much swearing and lurching I tried a few experimental steps, and to my amazement was eventually able to get moving again - as long as I kept the foot in a straight line everything seemed more or less OK.

Reassured, I continued and put in the planned two hours hard running and sat in the river when I got back to the car feeling very righteous.

Well, if it's going to flare it'll be after 1.5 hours on my arse in the car...

And so it proved.

I drove straight to my physio folks at The Body Rehab in Staveley, but by the time I got there I was in serious pain and rapidly becoming a danger to myself and other road users.

Tipping myself out of the car I dragged myself through the doorway and a short time later was sitting with my right foot strapped into a cryo-boot doing a very poor impression of a grown man in control.

I could see three months' dedicated prep going right down the tubes.

The gods however, had other ideas, and had sent me an angel called Roxy.

"I'm 99% certain it's an inversion sprain," she said. "But it's so swollen I can't be completely sure - it's off for an X -ray for you, young man..."

So followed 48 hours of intensive rest, ice, compression, elevation re-hab, then more work, then a half hour test jog with four days to go.

"I can't believe it," I reported to Roxy. "That all felt fine...what the heck did you do?"

The angel smiled. "We started treatment only five hours after the in-jury - early intervention makes such a difference - and you have been a very good boy with your homework..."

I get home and practically skip through the door.

Charlotte my wife raises a quizzical eyebrow.

"Well, am I packing my tent, or what?"

"Well, there is some more rehab to do..." I'm grinning like an idiot, "but we're on!"

Making The Complex Simple

The day after the race Family Mouncey are relaxing at Coniston race HQ with my great friend Geoff who ran the '50. We're catching up for the first time and comparing notes.

"So how was the race, Andy - really?"

"Completely consistent - no low points at all. I mean, the legs got in-creasingly trashed to the point where I sat in the river just before the Chapel Stile check...but other than that, mentally and emotionally I felt fine the whole way."

What went on in that head of yours then?

"Ah, that's easy - three words. Relax. Light. Smooth. And I thought about my family a lot - Charlotte and our two small boys - so lotsa happy faces there."

So internal focus the whole way?

"God, no. Switched in and out. Really relaxed during the night section. Adam (Perry) who I was running with and I did the 'torch off, have an 'ooo' moment at the moon above Braithwaite, for instance. Lots of moments like that."

It looked like you held second pretty much the whole way round - that looked like a pretty consistent effort.

Not quite. There was some chopping and changing in the early stages, and Duncan (Harris) got away on the Braithwaite section - didn't catch him again till halfway.

I ran this race completely differently from my other 100's.

At this race in 2008 I walked the first mile, and at Western States in 2004 I walked the first two!

This time I ran from the front 'cos my primary goal for the race was getting answers to three questions:

1. What does it take to run at the front?

2. Do you have what it takes?

3. Are you willing to make the commitment to find out?

So I was prepared to run hard to Wasdale - and I did. 'Ran the whole way and go out on record pace to get time and distance - especially as the other advantage I have is that I know where I'm going.'

I was also prepared to blow up - 'cos that would've still given me an answer.

I didn't think I would - but even if I did I also figured I could relax and regroup through the night.

I looked at it like this: with very few exceptions, everyone slows down over this distance - the issue is who slows down the least.

Out of sight really is out of mind - I just figured my 'slow' might still be good enough.

Unfortunately for me, Stuart (Mills- winner) had exactly this strategy and did it better than I did!

So that, really, was my race. No drama, no screaming and crying or flaying of undercarriage like 2008.

Solid, deliberate, thought-through.

Remarkably, as I said to Charlotte a few days later, this time it didn't even seem like such a long way. Now that is quite an adjustment.

I am however, all too well aware that a few short paragraphs don't really cut it from a race report perspective. Y'all want 'em coloured in don't you? Alright then, here it is...

Practising my game face at the start

Off The Front

So exactly what pace do you run the first 200 yards of a 100 mile race?

No-one except eventual winner Stuart Mills seems to know.

The race is thirty seconds old and already Stuart is out of sight having shot off the front from the start. For those who know him it's a tried and tested Mills tactic. Sometimes it works, and sometimes...

Well, he's either going to come back or he's not, I decide - no way am I following that!

I am however, going to do my thing which is to get moving in these first 20 miles or so, and as I don't especially want to run with anyone, I fix my gaze to the front and get on with it.

The first little descent gives me a clue - I'm faster than the two guys who have come past me on the climb out of Coniston - and once again I have my desired personal space and a periodic glimpse of Stuart as we head up the Walna Scar Road to the high point of the stage. I'm caught again before the top and this time joined by a new face. I recognise Duncan Harris (Fellsman winner) and we share a quick mutual appreciation of the glorious evening sunshine.

I redress the balance once again on the long descent down to the Seathwaite valley, but not before Duncan takes an almighty tumble in front of me - I mean, wipe out big style! I stop and check as he makes reassuring noises...but you really don't need a fall of that magnitude this early into this race. No matter, gravity tugs and I follow her lead. It feels awful fast and part of me flashes a warning light or two, but I figure that's just the girlie cautious part and key the manual over-ride.

Straight in and out of the first checkpoint stopping only to 'dib' and a bottle refill and into the woods around Wallbarrow at the head of the Dunnerdale valley. I'm dialled right in now and though I'm not wearing a watch, (and will not ask for time gaps till Ambleside) I know I'm on target pace which will mean 75 minutes to Boot. Relax. Light. Smooth.

I relax into the steep climb, running easily through the rocks, keeping half an ear open to voices and gate noises behind.

The action's ahead of you, Mounce...

I dance through the bogs and the rocky sections round the base of Harter fell with a confidence which comes with multiple recces.

A whispered 'thank you' takes me successfully past the site of my fall 10 days ago and I belatedly realise that there's been not a twinge from the ankle. Wow - maybe it really is gonna be OK...

Before long I'm cruising into Boot to the cheers of a handful of well-wishers outside the pubs. (I don't know it at the time, but I'm only two minutes down on my estimation. What I do know is everything's in the green and I'm grinning like an idiot. Having a good time? You betcha).

Another fast pit-stop at checkpoint two and onto the gradual climb out heading NE to Burnmoor Tarn above Wasdale. Still running, I clock voices behind me for the first time as we clear the tree-line and head onto the open fell. Ah, so there you are...

I spot a figure ahead and assume it's Stuart.

Fleeting delight turns sour as I close the distance and realise it's a lone walker. Stuart has well and truly gone - already eight minutes ahead by the Boot checkpoint.

A couple of miles later Duncan and Adam Perry get their chance to move ahead as I pull over for a pit-stop with miles of open moor for cover.

An apologetic "Sorry!" greets them as they run past. At least I've re-membered to squat in the 'cheeks away' position.

Once again I hook up with gravity and run fast to catch them before the final road section into Wasdale Head. Introductions all round.

"Sorry about the full moon back there," I say.

I find out later Duncan is surprised I'm back with 'em so soon.

I thought that would give you much more problems, he admits as we compare notes afterwards.

Nah, just a bowel movement. Sorry, fella.

We beat the checkpoint crew to the checkpoint.

Biting down the spike of frustration we get on with the job of being in and out of there sharpish and turn our faces to the first big climb up Black Sail pass.

Duncan forges ahead but by the time we're down the other side at the youth hostel we're back together.

A jog and power-hike up Scarth Gap and we're on the rocky drop to Buttermere.

Dance, man...

Relaxing & Recharging

Before long Adam and I are running easily along the western shore of a tranquil lake with Duncan some yards behind.

For the first time in 25 miles I can feel myself relaxing with the aggression-driven battle-grin being replaced with something much more serene.

As Adam and I do the 'commune with nature' piece I realise I am almost blissfully happy with where I am right now: at the front end of the race, running easily in the twilight along a beautiful silent lakeside with only our footfalls for company.

Getting here before full darkness has been a real bonus, and while the next section has a couple of tricky navigation sections, I am 100% confident can nail 'em first time.

I still haven't used my map or route notes - something I will continue throughout the race.

So I spend a few self-indulgent minutes putting big ticks against a few boxes.

I dally a little too long at the checkpoint, breaking my rule about no food stops till 30, 55, and 70 miles, but the chicken soup proves a draw too much - or I'm still away with the cosmic fairies...

This allows Duncan to catch us and be gone ahead of us into the darkness.

I'll see his headtorch twice more, but will only catch him again just before halfway.

I'm still not completely sure whether it's because I relaxed or Stuart and Duncan pushed on, but I see later that over the next two sections Stuart puts close on 20 minutes into me.

That's for later. For now, I'm a very happy boy moving at my own pace through the darkened fellside as Adam and I thread our way through the bracken NE to Braithwaite.

I separate myself from Adam as we drop into the village, and one rushed bowl of pasta and rice pudding later he still hasn't appeared at the checkpoint. I spot a headtorch circling as I head onto the Keswick road.

'Adam! Over here!' I can almost hear his sigh of relief. 'See you on the next section, fella.'

I spot his torchlight catching up as I climb through the switchbacks around Latrigg.

Relax. Light. Smooth.

It's still coming easily and I'm still scoring 11 on the Happy Scale.

Then on the dogleg around Lonscale Fell and Blencathra something strange happens.

I'm not looking but I swear I can feel Adam behind me.

'Won't be long now', I think, 'he's done well to catch up...'

Then nothing.

I get a chance to check for torchlight as I double back on the run-in to Threkeld, but again, nothing.

Next time I see Adam it's at Coniston on Saturday evening.

"I just blew big style," he told me, "had to lie down on the track. Managed to get to the checkpoint at Blencathra Centre, got some food down me, but had to go to sleep again. Then as there was nothing there I decided I had to get to Dalemain - so that's what I did - walked the next two legs." He paused while we all took this in.

"I'm a bit pissed off," he said, "Cos now I really will have to race in two weeks' time at Bradwell!"

That's all later. For now all I know it's back to me and my favoured personal space.

Making Ground

Something new happens over the next 28km as we head into daybreak and the 'halfway' point (actually 59 miles) at Dalemain on the north shore of Ullswater: I make time on Stuart. It's not huge and I'm still oblivious to relative progress being 'split-free' but I learn later it's enough to cause a few 'oos' and 'ahs' among the watching community as the live feeds come into race HQ.

What I do know is that everything's still working, and despite slowing over the final section I'm still moving along at a reasonable clip.

Remember, your 'slow' will still be good enough, man...

I get a massive boost as I spot Duncan for the first time through the trees with about 3km to go to the checkpoint. I get another injection as I can see he's looking behind him.

So I close to a couple of hundred yards. Then I sit there.

He solves the 'how / when do I pass him?' question by diving into the toilet just before the checkpoint proper.

(He tells me later he was feeling so rough that when he got through the checkpoint he crashed out on a bench somewhere in Pooley Bridge and really struggled through the next section. But he picked up something strong in the later stages and had closed a sizeable gap at 60 miles down to 20 minutes at the finish).

The problem is that I've stopped way too long at Dalemain and it takes me an age to get going again. It's a real exercise in patience and belief, and I'm talking to myself almost constantly on the couple of miles between Dalemain and Pooley Bridge.

I remember flying through this section in training imagining how revitalised I'd feel starting the final 40 miles.

Well, while my faculties are all there and firing: my trusty legs are somewhere else.

I do eventually get going again, heading down the eastern shore of the lake, but someone somewhere has registered that I've lost what feels like oceans of time on what should be a simple section.

Relax, man - your slow is still fast enough...

Let's hope so.

I vaguely remember someone telling me Stuart was about half an hour ahead at Dalemain, but I really wasn't listening so I'm not sure how accurate that was.

I do know, however, that he's not stopping for food - so whether it was half an hour or not, he'll be a damn sight further ahead by now.

Unless he's blown.

A business-like stop at Howtown and I set my face to climb up Fusedale Beck to the high point of the entire route at 655m with High Street off to the right.

This was where my world fell apart two years ago in driving rain, so I smile as I recognise that at least one thing will be different.

I climb strongly and get my lines nailed through thick bracken as I descend to the western shore of Haweswater.

And while I don't know it at the time, I make up my biggest chunk of time on Stuart and grab back all the time I lost between Dalemain and Howtown.

By the check at Mardale Head at 75 miles the gap is the shortest it's been since Braithwaite at 34 miles.

Back at race HQ the bets are being frantically re-made. Is this the start of a charge for the lead?

In a word: No.

This is as close as I'll get.

Reality Strikes

Stuart puts an hour into me over the final quarter as my legs become progressively less able to cash the cheques my brain is writing for them.

I'm still able to power-hike up the steep stuff and hold it together on the flats, but to my dismay I'm getting less and less able to run the descents.

My ankle is starting to give me the finger on the wobbly sections and a combination of recent heavy rain and footpath repair work has given us all horrible loose small rocks and big stones to travel over.

Throw in some wet stuff from the rain which has now set in and we've got one of the most user-unfriendly final 25 miles to cover.

And it's the same for everyone, Mounce, so shut the **** up and get moving. Remember, your 'slow' will still be fast enough...

Fast enough to hold second place, but I can feel my hoped-for 24 hours slip away.

By the time I hit Ambleside with 16 miles to go I know I've got a near-impossible task on my hands to hang onto a '24 time.

"How far ahead?" I ask.

"About 45 minutes" they tell me."But he looked way worse and he walked out of here."

That draws a snort: "Listen, I'LL be walking out of here!"

A sip of soup.

"45 minutes…someone's gonna have to shoot him, then."

Right then and there I consign all thoughts of a chase over this final section to the bin and turn back to paying attention to the internal indicators.

"Daddy, you're doing really great running just like me!"

The world is a delightfully simple place when you're three years old, and my emotional turbo-charge has been to meet the other members of Family Mouncey.

So while Tom races round the shop, I have time for a final hug with Charlotte and baby Joe.

"You look great, babe!" Her eyes are shining.

You just can't bottle it - so after tackling our racing toddler for a good-bye, I head out for what I regard as the final section.

And while it all feels slow I also know it's faster than two years ago, and that'll do, thanks very much.

I have a blissful beef stew moment at Chapel Stile and pause just to 'dib' at the last check.

"Sorry, gotta get on with it," I apologise to the crew.

There's nearly 1000' to climb over this last four miles or so and there's no time like the present. I allow myself my first look behind as I drop through the mines above Coniston just to make sure…then it's a very quiet jog through the rain back to where it all started one brief day earlier.

"Daddy, Daddy, Daddy - you're back!"

Tom cannons into me and I momentarily drop my composure all over the road.

I scoop him - and it - up, registering that it's my first real fumble in a day that has given me so much.

And yeah, I'll take it all, thanks.

"Daddy, Daddy, Daddy - you're back!"

Some Stats:

Total race distance: 104 miles / 6971m climbing & descending.

Andy finished 2nd in 25 hours 37 minutes

Total starters 123 / Total finishers 70

2011

Some unfinished business, a work in progress and a step above and beyond were the key pieces of my running year.

As to the rest, well, my business began to pick up again after three very lean years post-credit crunch, Tom started full days at school, and Joe turned two at Christmas. Family Mouncey was doing OK.

Unfinished Business was the Fellsman and the first big target of the year. I'd gone round very comfortably last year at first time of trying. This year that race had a big 12 hour target time on it for me and I was being much more thorough in my preparation. For the first time in many many years I'd engaged someone to work as coach/mentor with me.

All was going swimmingly till calf injury in April - had overcooked training: too motivated, too much, too fast and too uphill. Of course, I'd really done a good job on it which meant time off and big treatment. Struggling to get the balance right, the injury recurred twice more before early summer.

Work In Progress would be Lakeland 100 at the end of June - my third time on the start line having only missed one year of the race in 2009. A completely different approach this time from last meant I was less than bullish as the start approached. My diary records only eight races between January and August, and six of those came before the middle of May. The other feature of note was far less quality 'hard' training than previous years. Many of my normal indicators of progress were absent and I had committed to a race strategy I had last used in 2005. Nervous? You betcha.

A Step Above and Beyond would be my first visit to Ultra Tour Mont Blanc coming one short month after L100. I had NO idea how that would pan out but I was willing to give it a whirl after sampling the incredible atmosphere and mind-blowing landscape as a spectator last year.

I went into the autumn thinking that I'd really missed my racing this year, and that this ultra stuff is all well and good but it don't half make you slow if that's all you do. I resolved to do something about that and promptly bought a cyclo-cross bike. Before all that, the year kicked off with the annual sort-out of club bragging rights…

Winter Club Handicap Race 2011: First Blood

February, Settle Harriers at Clapham

Listen.

Can you hear it?

That's right - the thud of thrown gauntlets hitting the ground at the annual collision of running rivalries, egos and aspirations new and previous.

Welcome to the most keenly contested race of the year.

Welcome to my running club's winter race handicap.

Just under seven miles of muddy fields, rocky footpaths and a bit of fell thrown in for good measure before a heart-in-mouth plunging last descent over greasy rock which ends through two tunnels.

You heard me - tunnels.

Which means we hurtle down the last half mile on the edge of control to be plunged into darkness gritting our teeth and biting down the fear of turning an ankle in the rocky darkness as our eyeballs scream something along the lines of 'What the ****?!??!!

One thousand-two thousand-three thousand four-thousand and daylight - and then here comes the second one...

Oh yeah, and you'd better pray there's no walkers coming the other way.

Last year we had snow. Alex was chasing me down and I ran like a scared thing.

This year we have torrential rain and as defending champ I'm last one off.

This time I get to chase.

Warm up. Ha ha - that's a joke in this stuff - but I do it anyway on legs that tell me they still have Friday's mountain session in them. So I modify the plan to a steady start over the mud and then wind it up once we hit the better paths.

"3-2-1-go, Andy!"

Alex is 30 seconds up and my first 50 yards to the first stile is almost a sprint.

And so is the second. Uh-oh.

But I'm consumed with catching the long-striding figure in front who seems to be gliding over the glook. Very quickly I'm blowing big-style - but that's OK, it'll settle, stay with it - and reconcile myself to an uncomfortable first mile or so till it all kicks in.

But boy, am I blowing!

And despite the foul weather there's traffic today - big groups of walkers who part like the red sea as a series of mud-splattered heavy-breathing idiots hurl themselves through the stiles.

Remember to smile and say thank you...

Something vaguely audible emerges as I'd much rather use all the resources I have on more important matters because a few warning lights have started to flash - and the gap remains the same. "****!"

Here come the doubts. Has he gone off hard or is it me? ****ing hell I should be closing by now, shouldn't I?

Legs feel like lumps of wood, which requires serious teeth-gritting face-gurning to maintain what feels like any vague notion of speedy passage.

No worries, you've got the road section coming up. Relax, fly the downhill to the bridge and use the momentum to close up.

Which works fine except for one thing - Alex isn't in on my plan and gets further ahead.

More rude words my mum would not be proud of, but on this next flatter section as the bridle way twists and turns I know I need to keep the pressure on.

It'd be so easy to lose time as Alex will be frequently out of sight.

But it ain't pretty and it's hardly a zen-like model of free-flowing running either.

I'm focusing on stuff I absolutely can't control and it's killing me.

Briefly back on the road - where's..? Bugger.

No change. As Alex disappears into the start of the hilly bit I finally do what I should've done a while back: I let go the elastic and give myself a serious talking to.

Right. Settle down, focus in, you muppet. Just get through this next section and see. Remember the good session Friday - you can do this.

So I do.

Out of the woods over the stream and the landscape opens out.

Up ahead is a familiar gliding figure and he's...

Closer.

Alright. ****ing game on, then.

Head up, open stride and once again I use a slight downhill to up the cadence.

I'm still working like a good 'un but tell myself that if Al hasn't broken away on the climb through the woods then he isn't about to on the one coming up just around this corner.

Heck, it sounds plausible.

And sure enough we remain pegged and I use it to get a bit of a breather after my last charge along the bridle way. Alex knows the best lines as we thread around the fell and start to reel in more runners ahead. A few half-hearted grunts of greeting and vague awareness that I'm really being most impolite - but my entire world is just a few tens of yards ahead.

A final right turn over the gate and onto the bridle way which will take us through the tunnels and home.

I tell myself five more minutes max. Five minutes! C'mon you *****er - close this gap!

Finally the legs respond, (oh, now you decide to work, do you?) and I close and close.

"Well run, Andy"

John Oz has just been reeled in by Alex and is my final marker before the man himself.

I grit my teeth at the greeting thinking if Alex hasn't heard me coming, then he sure knows I'm here now - so bang goes the surprise pass.

If Al chooses to turn and look I've made it hard for him by sitting directly behind him about five yards down, and as we both charge for the top of the final descent I run through the options.

NOW!

I accelerate off a slight downhill, swing wide and open the throttle trying to get past as fast and as wide as I can.

No response - I'm clear!

KEEP GOING!

We swing left and right and then gravity calls and we drop down towards the waiting darkness. I'm caught between desperately trying to keep my footing and my speed, and to block out the sound of Alex's footfalls behind me.

Now is not the best time to remember how good he is over steep uneven ground.

HE'S GETTING CLOSER!!!!!

WALKERS AHEAD!

We're screaming towards the first tunnel mouth and now there's traffic ahead as well as the thunder behind me. If I don't brake I'm gonna...

BRAKE!

Flash past the bedraggled startled couple - sorry! - and into the darkness momentarily blinded and still flying.

STAY ON YER FEET - STAY WITH IT - STAY IN THE TRACK!

So easy to be freaked as my vision is ripped away and I'm still falling forwards through the stones - it's only for a few strides - hold on, boy!

*****ING HELL - ALEX! RIGHT BEHIND ME!*

At least that's what it sounds like as the tunnel plays its acoustical tricks.

Unfortunately I've forgotten that. Fortunately it scares the life out of me enough to give me a final kick as once clear of the second tunnel...

GO!!!!!!

Everything's a blur as I put everything else into getting rid of those damn footfalls.

Through more walkers, parked cars and out onto the final 100 yards of road.

It still ain't pretty and it's still gurning, but it IS working.

A final turn into the car park and I wobble over the finish line stuffing my lungs back down where they belong.

A turn and there's Alex.

A heartfelt handshake and river of mutual respect.

A big grin.

"Getcha next year."

An even bigger one back.

"You can try!"

Fellsman 2011:Racing

"Sticky clippers."

I raise a quizzical eyebrow around a mouthful of post-race trifle to the new Fellsman race record holder (10 hours 6 minutes for 62 miles and 11,000' climbing) sitting next to me.

"I beg your pardon?"

Jez Bragg tries again.

"Did you have any problems with sticky clippers?"

'Ah!' Realization dawns. "Now that you mention it - yes, I did."

So we'd hurtle in to the checkpoints, get our plastic race cards clipped, and want to be out of there sharpish. The only problem was that then the damn things required some serious wrist wrestling from the attendant marshal before they would disengage.

"So how much time do you reckon that was worth?"

Cue comedy sharp intake of breath.

"Gotta be five seconds a checkpoint...Heck, let's be generous - call it three seconds"

"5 seconds over 24 checkpoints..?" I can still do the maths so I'm clearly not that stuffed.

"That's over a minute and a half."

I look across at last year's UTMB winner who was just on another planet today.

A wicked grin: "That means you really did around 10.04 then...only FOUR minutes off a sub-10 time. That's pathetic, Jez - what on earth were you messing about at?!"

A chuckle. "And that sub-12 time you were after?"

A pause while that sinks in.

"Yeah, I know - I was robbed!"

***

Fellsman Start

400 yards into the race and I've already ripped up Plan A.

I know it's not big or clever - and I don't care.

After nigh-on six weeks up and down with injury and illness and three missed target races and a pre-Fellsman week of intense rehab, I'm finally running freely with not a twinge from the problem calves.

So I've quickly adopted Plan B - and Plan B, (subtitled 'Needless Indulgence') says I can run as I feel for this first bit, and sod the science.

As we start the first climb up Ingleborough I'm jogging happily along a few yards behind multiple winner Mark Hartell and someone else who has been racking up the trophies at home and abroad over the last few years, one Jez Bragg.

And there's silence behind me - I can't hear anyone.

Surely we haven't got a gap already, have we?

My 'eyes front' rule dictates I can't check this so I content myself with trying to stay relaxed and keeping space between the two champions ahead. There's a world of difference between running with them and just off them, and I'm quite happy in my own space, thank you.

I marvel at how smoothly Jez in particular is moving while he and Mark chat away in front. He seems to glide up the gradient, everything tidy, together, seemingly effortless. I recall racing with him at his first ultra in 2004 - heck, even I was young then!

We come together as the climb steepens and we're joined by Adam Perry. I'm genuinely delighted to see him - we ran together for many of the first miles of last year's Lakeland 100 and I haven't seen him since - so spend the next few minutes catching up between breaths.

With Adam Perry on the first climb up Ingleborough

But while I'm smiling inside and out and I'm well aware that I'm also running way ahead of a 12 hour schedule - that thing which sailed out the window after 400 yards.

"You're way ahead of schedule!" Mark calls back.

He should know - he helped me put it together.

"I know. You worried yet?" Like that's going to happen...

Chuckles all around. Heck, it's just fun to be out and playing, y'know?

The four of us make the summit together, and then gather for the plunge off the summit plateau.

The leading group nearing the summit of Ingleborough: Mark Hartell,
Jez Bragg, me, Adam Perry

"Mark missed a bus or something?" Jez is back with me after we all take a slightly different line.

"Nah - just got a good line down that steep bit with his extra grippy shoes."

Jez and I are watching Mr Fellsman open a 100 yard gap off the mountain.

Someone decides that's just not on and we race into the first checkpoint at Hill Inn for a quick bottle fill, our second sticky clipper moment, and shoot off down the road at what seems like a stupid pace.

For the first time in decades I'm racing wearing a watch.

This is consistent with Plan A: run to a schedule, check your splits, Andy.

As I'm now on Plan B, the watch now has a different role.

I'm not looking at the time, but I am recording the checkpoint splits for later analysis.

I know Mark will be on around a 10.30 pace (his course record stands at around 10.15) which will put us at Hill Inn in under the hour.

Which means I'm 6-8 minutes faster than I'm scheduled to be.

Ah.

But this is fun!

Part of me protests that this is still not big or clever, but a bigger part is still just very happy to be out and racing again - so let's just get on with it, shall we?

Together again on the climb up Whernside, and while Mark and Jez stretch out ahead by the summit, we're all together again as we start the drop into Kingsdale.

Suddenly Mark has pulled up and is right in front of me clutching the back of his leg.

What..? He's pulled something - oh no!

Now is not a time to make thoughtless remarks to the multiple winner of this race, but I want to say something as I move around him.

"It's a pull...?"

He mutters something around gritted teeth.

**** "Stay safe, Mark."

It's the best I can manage and it's fleeting at that. Jez has forged ahead to the checkpoint and I hurry to peg the gap - arriving as he's still filling bottles.

Again, we're both swiftly through and onto the climb to Gragareth.

And while I don't know it, my splits will show me later that I'm another 6-8 minutes up.

The elastic stretches on the climb. We cross on the short out and back to the summit. I have assumed an 'I'm still cool' face while Jez appears to be deep in ipod mode.

I'll get a glimpse periodically on the climb to Great Cowm, but for all intents and purposes he's gone.

A slight overshoot on the approach to the Great Cowm checkpoint - visions of Mark's unforced error last year - gives Adam the chance to close the gap we've had since the drop off Ingleborough, and we're together as we drop into Dent at about 20 miles.

Every action has an equal and opposite reaction

Or to put it in more succinct ultrarunning terms: cock it up and you'll get it back with interest - the only question is when and how much you get to pay.

At the checkpoint I trade calories for time and it's a mistake. I know it's a mistake, but I can't see any sandwiches ready and I don't ask for what I can't see. I scoot out of there with just an orange and full bottles to show for it, full of misplaced pride from another swift stop and that Adam is once again behind me.

The payback begins on the climb to Blea Moor. Adam goes past me with a cheery greeting as my world starts to implode.

For a few minutes it just doesn't occur to me to eat - I just can't figure why I'm slowing - then I try and get a Cliff Bar down my neck but I've got to practically ram it down with a pole - I do NOT want to eat that thing!

"****ing hell, I'm going down here!"

No ****, Sherlock.

Adam's reached the checkpoint and practically skips over the skyline and is gone. I, on the other hand, am dragging my sorry ass to the lone figure outside the tent, mumble a few words of greeting and walk listlessly off.

The happy camper of the first 20 miles picturing a smiley fast finish in Threshfield is gone. In his place is a wobbling shell who is now struggling to get his head around arriving at half way. I am entertaining all kinds of thoughts about calling it a day:

You don't really want this...

It's not that important...

It's OK, you've been injured...

Those legs feel really sore, don't they...

You could stop at Stonehouse and get a lift back easy...

Remember after Redshaw and halfway you're committed...

Bullshit - the lot of it.

Finally some sense breaks through the wallowing self-pity, and I do what I should have been doing all along: reduce the size of the chunks I'm focused on.

Just get to Stonehouse, get some food down you and see...you're still moving and you can still see Adam...it's all downhill from here...just get off the moor and onto the road - you can f***in' roll down from there...

It's a pathetic descent, but it is a descent and that means I'm getting closer to the checkpoint. Once I hit the road it's a gradual half mile or so downhill to sanctuary, and to my relief I drop down a few notches on the pathetic scale.

OK...you can still move then...

It's the fastest pasta demolition job you are likely to see this side of civilization, and while I'm still not Mr Happy, neither am I entertaining thoughts of binning it right here. Adam is still here on shovelling detail as well so I figure either he's on for a serious scoff, or I haven't dropped quite everything all over that last section of the course.

I set my thoughts to the imminent climb and jog out in Adam's wake.

A run-walk combination up to the final push up Great Knoutberry keeps the distance between us pegged and my morale gets a boost, but once onto the open moor and into the wind on the out and back to the trig point, I am back to grovelling patheticness.

My world reduces down to the three metres in front of me as Adam forges ahead into the wind. This section has hurt and even on the descent I'm slow - half-clocking the familiar faces behind me and estimating gaps.

Because there still is quite a big one behind me.

By the time I hit halfway I can see Adam already some distance beyond the checkpoint. The gap has really stretched this time.

And while I'm not doing 'fire-in-the-eyes-gonna-getcha', neither am I entertaining any real thoughts of calling it a day.

Get some more food down you, keep moving, let's just see...

Ahead is a chance to make some ground, taking a direct route to the gate on the Cam High Road. To my delight I see the distant figure of Adam following the wall on what I am convinced is the long way round.

A rictus grin and I go direct - time to get some time back! - get my lines nailed and emerge.

No-one in sight. Nothing behind and nothing ahead.

Gotcha!

Then I look again, and in the distance about to disappear on the approach to Dodd Fell is a lone figure.

Adam - and he's gained a bucketload of time.

I'm momentarily crushed - I was convinced that mine was a quicker line - but right there before me is undeniable evidence to the contrary.

I retreat back into my cave, and though I'm moving reasonably well, there's nothing remarkable about it at all. I arrive at Fleet Moss just as Adam is leaving. A shouted greeting and I register he's going for the direct route.

Okayyyy...that's interesting...

I'm swift through the checkpoint and head out on the runnable southern route which skirts the moss. My pace and focus pick up, helped by periodically clocking Adam ahead. He seems to have ditched the direct route and emerged not too far ahead of me. The gap is closing. I get my lines spot on and close some more up to the blue mug stile.

He tells me later he slowed over Yockenthwaite Moor and the approach to the new checkpoint. It shows as well. The entire field is on new ground with this 11th hour course change, and there's no use in looking for Jez's footprints. He was, I remind myself, floating anyway. I put my faith in map and compass and arrive at the new checkpoint the closest I've been to Adam since Blea Moor.

Then it's choice time: direct over difficult ground to the newly-moved Hell's Gap checkpoint or go for the handrail, which is a wall to the south, and hope for more runnable terrain if slightly longer.

I made my choice before the start, so as Adam heads direct I go for the wall. To my delight there is indeed a small path on the north side - it's a relief to be able to run smoothly again after jog-walk-stumble across the lumpy, broken, peaty, heather-strewn moorland.

I emerge onto the Cray track about 200 yards south of the checkpoint just as Adam runs past en route to Cray.

OK, so that kinda worked...

Quickly up to the checkpoint to give the marshals a scare ('Where the heck did you come from?!') and back the way I've just come.

Again, it ain't speedy, but it ain't pathetic either - and someone somewhere registers that I've still been putting in a respectable pace over these last few sections.

Someone also registers that it's still very much daylight, and my goal for a daylight finish looks very much on.

Another swift checkpoint - that has been a feature this time - and I'm girding myself for the steep pull up Buckden Pike. It's blowing a gale on top but I figure as we're not up here for long it's best to keep plugging away. I cool down frighteningly fast which only serves to add urgency into my traverse of the summit plateau.

The plunge off into warmer stuff is much appreciated - though the clocking of the fact that Adam has once again stretched the elastic, is not.

Park Rash checkpoint. The start of the final climb of the race up Great Whernside. Last year I was grouped here with six other runners in readiness for the onset of darkness. A little victory grin creeps out at the realisation that this year will be different.

The climb feels long, and I'm not betting much on the turbo boost effect from a couple of cocktail sausages grabbed at the checkpoint. I've opted for another swift stop and just get on with it, consuming from my own supplies.

Emerging once again into the teeth of the wind I'm buoyed by the thought that once I'm down off this baby, then there really only is the run into the finish. Not short, for sure - but flat.

I'm required to pull over for a pit stop on the descent, and while in full moon pose, my little world with just little me in is shattered as first lady Nicky Spinks glides by.

Where the f..?!?

As I've been doing 'eyes front' all the way the last time I saw what was happening behind me was the out and back of Great Knoutberry.

She is, I belatedly realise, running a perfectly paced race.

Hurriedly assuming the vertical position once again I'm once again allowing someone else to dictate my race. But I need some information quickly:

How's she moving?

Can I catch her on the steep stuff?

How's she going over the flatter ground?

Was that a burst she put in to get past me, or..?

I am indeed catching her on the steep stuff - but that's all.

Holding the gap on the flatter ground is requiring some serious focus and heavy breathing. I am acutely aware that I'm right on the edge between holding and blowing - and there's still a few miles to go yet.

The elastic stretches.

F***!

I'm not willing to raise it to what will be around a 40 minute sprint to the finish. Half that - who knows - but at the checkpoint at the foot of Great Whernside I pull my focus back on me.

The elastic snaps.

And then it's just about holding on. A serious wobble has me delving into my sack for emergency mint cake about half a mile from Yarnbury - after remembering to do so out of sight behind a gate from anyone behind me.

Yarnbury checkpoint - about 20 minutes running left.

"You're on for a sub 12 finish!"

I partly register it, but really am just locked into holding my form on the long level road section before the drop into Grassington, and am concentrating like crazy.

Once it drops, then you're close. Hold on, fella - relax - run tall...

Grassington at dusk, and there's no sound of thumping footsteps descending behind me.

Hold on...

Over the river and up into Threshfield I finally look behind me: Nothing.

A grin. There's the school.

"Runner finishing!!" The finish desk is choked with runners just off the pick up bus registering their DNF. I crank up the volume and give it another go.

Cue elbows and more shouting.

Tally clipped, wrestled away and clock stopped: "What's the time?!?"

A pause.

"12.00.35"

F***!!!!!!

The Lakeland 100 2011: Back To Front

"I really hope this works, Andy…"

15 seconds into the race and Co-Race Director Marc Laithwaite appears to be having doubts about where he's placed his bets this year. The reason? Last year's second placer - that's me, dear reader - has just walked past him right at the back of the field, appearing not to have a care in the world as the rest of the 233 runners stream away from the start.

I find out later that he was not alone in the raised eyebrow department. A whole bunch of folks did a big collective 'What the f***?!?!'

Bless 'em - but they didn't know what I knew: I had a plan, and I was working the plan. It was just that that plan was the exact opposite to last year's.

Now that's more like it! Race start 2011

Truth be told, it wasn't quite as straightforward as that. I wanted to take in the experience of the start - much more support here this year with the bigger field - and I needed a walk to let some emotions bleed out. You see, I'd prepared for a stack of scenarios in advance of this race, but there was one that took me completely by surprise: The number of people who greeted me pre-start with words along the lines of:

We're rooting for you, Andy.

This is your year, mate.

We really want you to do it this time.

Back at the tent I sit down very quietly feeling quite humbled by the whole experience. Charlotte looks at me in that wife way and I tell her.

A huge smile and a hug is her response: "But that's because we all love you and just want you to do well!"

"I know that, but - oh, bloody hell!"

This would all have been fine except for one teeny weeny detail: I'd had an almost completely different prep period for this race than I'd had for my previous two outings. The length of my specific training period and the content of that was, well, like nothing I recognised. Some of that was by chance and some of it was by design.

A result was that many of my usual indicators of readiness were missing - which meant I really had no clue as to my condition. I mean, I figured I was in OK shape - but how that actually translated? 'Might as well ask the audience'.

Except this audience clearly expect me to deliver a win - and nowhere in The Plan did it mention the word 'win'.

But you're not going to let these people down, now are you?

Er...'get back to you on that one, can I?'

So I needed the walk 'cos there was a bunch of re-framing to be done before Mr Fridge was back in control.

So I walked, looked, took it all in, and went to work on the inside stuff. And I actually thought I held it together quite well as there were indeed a few wobbly bottom lip moments.

And all that in the first 200 yards. Jeez! I've got a night and day of this stuff yet!

But it's a good plan for a goal that has taken me a long time to be at peace with.

The Plan - like any good plan, was simple:

Start at the back.

Walk the first bit.

Keep it relaxed, easy and in your bubble all the way to Howtown (65miles)

Fast through the checkpoints.

Walk anything that's vaguely uphill.

Use the poles from Howtown on the climbs.

You can start racing at 65 miles.

The Plan got underlined and refined at Race Briefing after a few words from none other than special guest Joss Naylor:

'Keep it relaxed, easy,' said the great man.

'Enjoy it and stay in the present.'

Relax, easy, be in the present.

Gotcha.

And The Goal?

Finish, having run as even a pace as you can. Do it right and it should only get interesting in the final third/quarter. One out of two people DNF this race, so a finish is special. Remember that. Anything else is a bonus. Finish with a run and a smile. Your boys need to see you happy and making good on a commitment - so finish.

Past the pubs in Coniston and equilibrium is returning. I'm chugging along quite happily in the late afternoon sunshine, already starting to weave through the field. Sometimes chatting and fielding the occasional 'But aren't you..? And shouldn't you be..?' but mostly quiet taking in the scenery and the sights and sounds of being at the back.

So this is what it all looks like from here...

The first plummeting descent from 600m to the valley floor and the first hiccup. I'd not laced my shoes up tight enough and the result was feet sliding around inside the shoes. I can feel hotspots developing under the heel of each foot. Not good. Pull over off the track and sort it out as everyone I'd left on the descent come past. Oh well...

The second hiccup comes two thirds of the way into the second leg as we skirt Harter Fell en route to Eskdale. There's a sharp descent and at the bottom is a sharp left turn. I've done this countless times in recces and races...and I miss it completely and go straight on, bringing a few folks with me. Fortunately I realise my mistake quite quickly and back-track to a chorus of heckling deriding my assumed route knowledge. I have the good grace to wince audibly. Sorry chaps.

Right, so all this 'relaxed - easy' is fine, but not so relaxed and easy that you're asleep. This is a competitive outing. Can we please pay attention as well?

Heading into Wasdale at around 19 miles and everything is very much in the green. I smile as I remember how swiftly I was moving by comparison last year at this point in the company of Adam Perry and Duncan Harris. Duncan is missing today but Adam is here and I expect him to be somewhere up the front. That's for later - for now I chug into the checkpoint and swiftly out again leaving behind a handful of folks in the process but not before I fail to block someone telling me I'm in 7th place. It's the last thing I want to hear.

7th place. What the heck am I doing in 7th already? This is waaaaay too early. Oh well...

I 'black-bag' that piece of information and set my sights on the upcoming lumpy bit. Two serious climbs and descents totalling 750m that will take me into Buttermere. I'm making a serious effort to relax on the climbs in contrast to last year. I've worked on my walking and my power-climbing so I figure I should be able to climb respectably without busting a gut. It seems to be working. I pass a stricken Ian Bishop part way up Black Sail who is wobbling all over the place after a fall. Help is ahead of him and he seems determined to make it. I can only wish him well as I head off.

So that makes it 6th, then...

The headtorch comes out at the start of the final descent down to the shore of Buttermere - bit earlier than last year then, son - and the start of periodic toe-stubbing stumbles which will trash my feet by the end.

There's just no two ways about it, it HURTS. It really does. Even if it doesn't floor you - which adds bashed shoulders, knees, hips, elbows, hands to the inventory - it will progress from tiresome-uncomfortable to seriously pissing you off and a trigger for language your mum would be appalled by. Cumulative effect? Oh, it's lovely!

Night-time is also a great opportunity to see who has the headtorch discipline nailed down.

Good Practice Tip No 1

When turning round to either check the view or the opposition, always turn your torch off or cover the light with your hand.

I'm constantly amazed by how many people don't do this. Might as well fire off a flare and scream 'I'M HERE!!' There are few things more encouraging in a night section than being able to see where folks are ahead of you - particularly if they've been out of sight during daylight.

Tonight it seems I am blessed because on a night with no moon - so it was black out there, really really black - I can see some twinkles ahead as I thread my way through the bracken-dense hillside towards Braithwaite.

And a very bright twinkle (two people?) is close.

Sure enough as I near the top of the high point for the stage, two lights come into view just below me.

Ah, missed that last turn then...

It spurs me into making the most of the pass, and without increasing effort I focus on a smooth descent and spot-on nav down what is a steep, rock-strewn path with a crucial navigation section in order to hit the correct exit line.

I'm completely in the groove, feeling effortless and grinning like a loon as I dance through the darkened hills. Into the checkpoint for the first serious feed.

4th then and just over one third of the way in...

I have a very happy, peaceful night section. It's dry, warm, the stars are out and it's all about me. My internal jukebox offers up some 80s classics while I break off periodically to check the 'relax-easy' dials.

Climbing up to the Old Coach Road at around 45 miles at the top of Threlkeld Common will be the start of four miles or so of undulating open stony track. I've learned to just relax into this because otherwise it can feel endless - doubly so in the night with little/no references to provide perspective and a sense of progress.

As the hillside opens out ahead I am rewarded with my first objective measure of the runners ahead of me - headtorches: one very faint and about to disappear out of sight, the other - no, wait, that's two close together - much closer.

Well hello, boys...

I play the guessing game - half an hour to the lead torch? (I'm wrong, because the splits later will show Terry Conway is around 40-50 minutes up at this point and going away with every stride) and 10-15 minutes to the pair (which is more like it).

Once that's done I file it under 'Future Action', close the file and pull my focus back to me and right now. Sister Sledge start up on the jukebox and normal operations resume.

Dawn finds me contouring round the western shore of Ullswater heading for Dalemain House and the 59m checkpoint commonly referred to as 'halfway.' It's my second section that has bordered on 'blissful.' It's quiet, still - there's just been no wind at all during the night - and I'm still in my bubble chugging along. The views afforded from this hillside path around Gowbarrow Fell are to die for, and I'm thoroughly enjoying treading the twisting undulating singletrack I've not seen in 12 months.

Dalemain. There's the tent and there's... 'Mr Perry - Good Morning!'

Adam and Paul Tierney are doing their thing at the checkpoint and I shout a greeting. I don't know it at the time but the splits will show later that I've closed significantly over these final few miles. The splits will also show that I'm only around five minutes slower to this point than I was last year. And last year I was at record pace for the first quarter or so and then was just trying to hold it together. I remember my legs being pretty stuffed and I took an age here and miles and miles to get going again afterwards. It really wasn't pretty.

What I do know is that 2nd and 3rd are still here which to my mind means either they've just arrived, or they're lingering - either of which is good news for me.

And my legs feel great.

With hindsight, this was my best chance to make the pass and get ahead of Adam and Paul, but it never even entered my head at the time. I was fixated on a shoe change, pole collection and big feed – and my plan was to start playing at Howtown. And the plan was working, this wasn't Howtown, and I was sticking to the plan.

We're into 'what if' territory and the hard and fast reality is that I'll never know whether trading food and kit change time here would have avoided all the fun and games which were to come later. Whatever. But for sure there's a lesson here about A Plan versus Flexible Response...

I remove myself to the opposite end of the checkpoint, make my food order and get business-like with my drop-bag.

Sit down, ditch the torch, grab the gel flasks, poles and shoes. I've decided on a shoe change just to change the pressure points on my feet. It's very dry and the forecast is for hot stuff today. I've no blisters but I want the security and relief of worn shoes and a slightly bigger size. I'm quick with the kit, secure the poles for action from the next checkpoint then focus on getting some hot calories down my neck as Adam and Paul get ready to leave.

My already high spirits are threatening to go orbital and I have to give myself a serious talking to while shovelling chocolate cake and custard down my neck.

Calm down, you've still gotta relax on this section. Pay attention, let's see how they're doing, and stay behind them. Plenty of time to decide how you're gonna do this. Stay with the plan, man...'

So I do.

The elastic stretches and shortens periodically over the next seven miles as we all head to Howtown on the other side of the lake. I'm still operating my bubble but this time the forward sensor suite is deployed. I notice a few things.

They're moving as a pair and running well over level ground.

I'm catching them on the climbs.

They appear to be less than sure about the route-finding.

It all gets filed but this time the file is staying open...

Howtown. 65 miles in and I can't wait to play. We all coincide at the checkpoint and I assemble my weapons. The 'to pole or not to pole' question has interested me for a couple of years now, and in that time I've gone from sceptic to 'it's not for me but I can see some value' to the 'sod it - I really need to figure this out.'

So I've had some serious pole-time as part of my prep for this race. The result is that I'm now a fan of the featherweight variety which collapse down into four sections (Mountain King Trailblaze), and I've decided to use them for this latter part of the race. We head out of the checkpoint 200 yards apart with me trailing and set our sights on the steep climb to the high point of the race at 665 metres.

Tapping out a great rhythm, I steadily close and we come together about a third of the way up as Adam and Paul pause to check directions. I march straight past.

"We're good, fellas - this is the path."

I crack straight on feeling great as we get onto the long steep stuff. As I make the crest before the final approach to the actual high point I catch a glimpse in my peripheral vision of Adam and Paul right behind me.

Time to try an experiment, then...

There's a key route choice right here and I need to see how confident they really are. So I stop and slowly stash my poles waiting to see what happens.

The boys have stopped a few yards away and are in conference.

I leave it a few more seconds more just to be sure, get up and walk to the correct path.

"This one, fellas."

I jog away and my mind is made up: I need to drop them on this next section otherwise they'll be able to tag me all the way to the next checkpoint at the head of Haweswater at 75m.

Paul I don't know, but Adam I do and have raced him on two previous occasions. Our score is 1-1. He's talented and tenacious and I like him tremendously.

But today we're racing and I need to break this elastic.

A footbridge some way ahead is a critical feature to hit en route to the shoreside path on the western side of the lake. The approach is down a steep bracken-covered hillside. There is a maze of paths and trogs all now hidden by waist-high lush bracken.

After two previous L100 races and many recce trips I now know the perfect line through the maze - and can find it even when it's hidden. I'm betting that Adam and Paul don't and can't - and I don't intend to hand it to 'em all gift-wrapped and lovely.

It's the perfect place to make a break - but I need to manoeuvre them in front of me in order to pull it off.

One small problem: There's no cover up here. No trees, rocks, anything to disappear behind. It's just open moor and on a day like today you can see for miles.

So this ain't going to be subtle.

A fierce grin at the prospect of what could be a crux move. Sorry boys, I just don't do freebies when I'm racing...

Note: *what follows is a genuine account of my head games. I am sure Adam and Paul have a slightly different perspective, but my self talk is my own and constructed for my benefit. It helps me to believe in this stuff and to me it's all plausible - and I really have no idea what Adam and Paul were actually thinking. All I knew was they were in front of me and I wanted to reverse that.*

I pull over, kneel down and fiddle with a shoelace.

Adam and Paul come past and move slowly ahead. The track is really faint here and I recall the first time I did this trip - not very sure at all...

Hmm, need to get further on where it firms up...

Ahead again. Stop for the other shoelace. Wait.

No joy.

Back moving but even though we're all still pretty close together, Adam and Paul are ahead.

Then Adam stops for a fiddle of his own which has me nearly breaking out in a fit of giggles at the comic cat and mouse routine that's going on here.

He's sussed what I'm up to - he must have!

So what. I'm staying right here and you boys are going on ahead...

I stop for a piss and for good measure un-ship my rucksack. And wait.

The path is now visible as far as we can see ahead. We're all moving once again and Adam and Paul are starting to jog away.

I resolutely stay walking and will them onwards, doing my Jedi mind-trick thing.

This is the path you're looking for...move along now...

Weird Jedi stuff or not, Adam and Paul are gathering speed and heading into the distance. I follow and give them 100 yards, 200 yards then make a break to the right, running hard down the flank of the hill to get out of sight. I'm now behind and below them and going like stink to get to the top of the bracken field before they can see me again. I figure even if they clock me in a sea of bracken they still have to figure my entry point.

I nail my lines and hit the bridge. My 'eyes-front' rule means I have no way of knowing what's going on behind, so I do the only thing I can - keep going to make the final drop to the shoreline and invisibility as fast as I can. I scream around rocks, holes and into yet more bracken-parting stunts and I finally drop onto the shoreline path breathing harder than I've done for any of that previous 15 hours or so. Just in case they're right on me I give it a little extra for a while because out of sight can really be out of mind in this game.

And then back comes the bubble. I key 'easy-relaxed' and the Spice Girls start to sing. It's a long pull round the lake, but all the indicators are in the green and as the clock ticks on to around sixteen and a half hours I trot into the checkpoint at Mardale Head at 75miles.

Terry is on another planet ahead, but the splits will tell me later I've put 10 minutes onto Adam and Paul during that stage to put me in 2nd place.

All I have to do now is hold it for the final 29 miles...

The monster climb out of the valley up Gatesgarth is followed by an equally monster descent and then another big pull and drop before the next checkpoint at Kentmere. The footpath repair schemes have meant that fresh supplies of large stones and small rocks have been dumped on what is already a loose difficult rocky path. It's a horrendous surface to negotiate if you're trying to do so with any degree of urgency - and has seemed to me to get worse every year. But my weapons of choice are coming into their own, helping me tap out a great rhythm and keep a good efficient posture. It's like keying the turbo-boost and I bless my decision to use 'em. The drop down the other side to Sadgill is measured, and as the sun starts to really burn I start to look forward to seeing my friends Phil and Annie at Kentmere.

I arrive at the checkpoint to a skeleton crew and am momentarily non-plussed. Wasn't this place jumping last year? Also there is no sign of my friends. I deflate a little more - after a long time solo I realise I'd been quite looking forward to this, especially as the edges of first real tiredness are starting to set in. A big inward sigh and I attend to the practicalities and am out of there sharpish. Ahead and Terry is now nearly two hours ahead, but behind me the gap has stretched to nearly 13 minutes...

Topping out on Garburn pass with my weapons of choice

Garburn Pass: Another loose rocky monster of a climb, but at the end of this leg is Ambleside at 88 miles and Ambleside means Family Mouncey. I allow some leakage and fantasize about seeing our boys and Charlotte. Big smiles inside and out soften the early stages of the climb, but very soon full Attention To Task is required.

Three figures ahead by the side of the track and two of them are...Annie and Phil, Mr and Mrs Alpine-Oasis. A fierce grin around a brief but heartfelt greeting. Phil is on film duty for race sponsors Montane and is snapping away like the seasoned trained professional he is. Run ahead, stop, turn and do the fast multiple shutter thing as I march past. Run ahead, stop, turn and do it all again. While I'm concentrating like crazy, part of me wonders how long Phil will keep this up - not all the way to the top, surely?

Yep - all the way up the 450m. By that point I am barely registering his herculean feat as I'm consumed by pulling off one of my own. My pace hasn't slackened but it's requiring more of me to hold it together. Phil's shouted farewell 'I'm loving your work, Mister!' sends me jogging over the top and then it's wits-about-you stuff for the descent. Another pole-assisted pull gets me overlooking Ambleside. Before long I'm chugging along the High Street searching ahead for the first sign of Charly and the boys.

Heading up the road to the Ambleside checkpoint at 88 miles.

And then they're there. Tom (4) jumping up and down in excitement with Joe (19 months) waving frantically in Charly's arms. 'Hi babe!' Kisses, smiles and hugs all round. But while the happy score is off the scale I'm also now very tired indeed. Worse, I don't fancy anything to eat from the selection on offer and settle for a cup of tea.

"How far ahead?" I ask Charly. It's the first time I've asked on the leader.

She waves a hand dismissively. "Oh, long gone - hours."

Oh. The subliminal message is clear. Forget him - focus on you.

Meanwhile our eldest is chatting away much to my delight and the amusement of the checkpoint crew. I give him some attention around my slurps as I get the run down on his day so far.

Charly tells me later she can see I'm really tired - I'm a little bit all over the place and my eyes have a hint of thousand yard stare in them.

"Just finish. You're doing great..." (she's smart enough not to tell me the time) "Look after yourself. We want you back safe and sound, remember?"

I remember. More hugs and kisses and time to go. It's another brief stop while behind me the gap is holding.

The final three stages have hint of death-march. I'm not dying but it's taking EVERYTHING I have to stay chugging along. I recall it felt slow, but here's the thing: running the numbers afterwards (I did not wear a watch or ask for time checks throughout) and a very different story emerged. I was significantly faster over all three final stages than last year, and even widened the gap on Adam and Paul until the final leg. My goal of 'even pace' is holding up.

I'm also burning up in the fierce sun to the point where I say 'f*** it!' and go and do a dead starfish impression in the river by Chapel Stile for a few minutes - much to the bemusement of the tourists. Full submersion is pure bliss and the reset button has been successfully keyed.

Out of the river and back on the road. Holding it together - just.

Tilberthwaite checkpoint and four miles to go. For the first time at a checkpoint I sit down and close my eyes as waves of fatigue wash through me. 'Time me for 30 seconds, will you?' I ask the crew. I know I need to get going, but sitting and sleeping feel wonderful. I've not been able to get anything down me except a few chunks of Kendal mint cake since Ambleside and a few mouthfuls of soup at Langdale. Part of me thinks it might be a good idea to eat something. The other part of me figures it's just too much like hard work. The checkpoint crew are totally on the ball and fantastically encouraging and I prise myself upright for the final time.

I crawl nearly on hands and knees in slow motion up the final murderous climb. I do get going again at the top and I need to. Adam and Paul will halve the gap between us on this short final leg. I tread a careful final descent and then it's a very, very weary trot down the track to Coniston village. Still doing 'relax-easy' and still holding the finish images at bay, I tell myself I can do the finish-fantasy bit when I hit the houses.

Right, left and 200 yards to go and, as last year, here comes Tom racing towards his Daddy. I remember dropping my composure all over the road at this point 12 months ago, but this time I'm just too tired. I'm barely able to pick him up for a welcome hug and have to put him back down again. He charges off while I wobble towards a very happy wife and waving baby. Big hugs and shining eyes, then all that remains is for Tom and I to do the finish line bit. 2nd again. So yeah, Marc - it really, (nearly) worked.

Footnote

I was completely oblivious of my time and splits throughout. I ran it blind. When Charlotte told me '24-27' a few minutes after I finished I was shocked. If you'd have asked me to guess I'd have said, 'er, 26ish?' My time gave me a 70 minute improvement on last year and The Plan gave me a consistently faster final quarter. Something to think about, then...

24 hours 27 minutes. Oh my goodness.

Ultra Trail du Mont Blanc 2011: DNF

'Bravo!'

'Courage!'

Late morning on Saturday and the Italian ski town of Courmayeur looks every inch picture-postcard under clear blue skies. I've just cleared the forest after a mind-bogglingly long and steep zig zag descent into what is the traditional half way point of the race after what has been for me nearly 12 hours of physical and emotional ups and downs on a truly alpine scale.

We've also had every type of weather thrown at us during the previous 78 km and some 4400m of climbing and descending, but that's not the reason for my haunted expression. It's because I know that my race will stop right here.

I've known that for the last few hours - it's just that the Italians are not making it easy. Men, women, young and old are out on the race route shouting and clapping encouragement to the weary runners. It's the children - the bambinos - that get to me, doing unbridled enthusiasm as only they know how. Thinking of my own boys just makes it worse and I feel the tears start to bubble. Then the UTMB race organisation works a leverage trick of their own. Every runner has their full name and the flag of their country printed alongside their number. The result is that spectators can make it personal. So I have my name shouted by smiling faces as I close in on the municipal sports complex in the centre of town which is the checkpoint. I feel a complete and utter fraud. My number is shouted ahead so that my dropbag with spare kit in can be found among the other 2299, and then the knife goes in. I'm handed it by a smiling young Italian boy not much older than my eldest: 'Bravo, Andy!'

Oh, Jesus...

I have to turn away as I'm in serious danger of bursting into tears right there, and walk the final few yards into the building trying desperately to smile and wave my thanks around a very wobbly bottom lip.

Up the stairs guided by kindly Italians and into what looks like a huge mess hall where runners are seated setting new speed records in food consumption. I look for the chair furthest away from everyone and everything and make a beeline for it. As I sit down the dam bursts and the tears flow uninterrupted for what seems like many minutes. It's taken 25 years of racing but finally I have another first: Mouncey, Andy, UTMB 2011, Did Not Finish.

Is This Wise?

It all started a week ago as I flew out early to get ready to receive the six runners I'd be coaching who'd signed up with www.alpine-oasis.com/ trail-running for a week in UTMB country.

"Andy, is this wise?" Phil and Annie (Mr & Mrs Alpine-Oasis) could, I suppose, be forgiven their scepticism.

Four weeks earlier I'd had the small matter of the Lakeland 100, then I was proposing to complete UTMB on the back of an intensive week in the mountains with a client group. While the pace over the ground would be very comfortable for me, it would be full-on in all other aspects.

So honestly? I didn't know. And I wanted to find out. And I was OK with it not going to plan to get my answer. But I also figured a week in the big stuff would be good for the legs and the head - because adjusting to the sheer scale of the landscape out here is one of the hardest initial challenges. So I'd built a case and presented my arguments - but the jury was still out.

Taking A Look

Before the clients arrived I had a route recce to complete.

"If you do nothing else then look at the final two climbs," said Mr Fellsman Mark Hartell. (There are 10 in total, by the way). "They're the steepest and the hardest and will make or break your race."

I only had time for a look at the final one, and realised very quickly that Mark wasn't kidding. It was a 700m monster all gained in 4km. Visions of grown men crying...

The Week Before

We had a superb week with our multi-national group of runners out and about from our base in Les Contamines on the UTMB race route. The sun shone as we introduced our folks to the joys of a glacial melt-water river bath post-run, English puddings, and a dog called Pickle. We also did some very cool running - culminating in an overnight stay at the high mountain refuge on the Croix de la Bonhomme - the high-point of the race route.

Then on the Monday our special guest Stuart Mills www.ultrastu. blogspot.com arrived, and a greater contrast in pre-race routines you could not find.

"Andy, is this wise?" intimated the man who beat me by about five miles at the 2010 Lakeland 100.

Well, at least it gave me another chance to rehearse my argument. Heck, it sounded plausible - didn't it?

Stu was a big hit - not least because his approach to this ultra lark is not the most conventional you will ever find, and therefore just perfect for busting some limiting beliefs and kicking off an argument - er, I mean, provoking discussion.

He was asked about his strategy: 'Go off as fast as I can while I can.'

Er, but it's a 100 mile race, Stuart - why would you do that?

"Cos it's fun to race the big boys."

It's fun??

I could see jaws dropping and eyebrows heading upwards, but there was no denying it, Mr Mills' enthusiasm was catching.

What about stretching, Stuart?

"I don't enjoy it so I don't do it - why would I do something I don't enjoy?"

Pause. Fair point.

Bombshell

Friday morning and a bomb drops as 2300 runners receive the following text from the race organisation:

UTMB: important storm + cold weather + rain or snow. UTMB start at 11.30pm

Phil has been watching the weather closely over the last 48 hours and this is the one he's been waiting for. Clearly the race organisation do not want a repeat of last year - race stopped three hours in due to awful weather - and do want to get the leading edge of the front out of the way before the race starts. But they've also taken the final climb out of the route in favour of a valley bottom option because the snow line is now down to around 2000m and the forecast is for seven shades of hell to sweep the high ground.

A five hour delay - so most people will do two nights then...

As 2300 race plans implode, I check the obvious first. Can I still make my flight home ??!

And then the rest of the day is given over to Plan B. I'm quite fortunate because I didn't have much of a Plan A to start with so there's really not much to change other than take advantage of the additional sleep and eat time. I do, however, change to more grippy shoes. For those runners who'd done the detailed scheduling, modelling and recce runs it was a different story - and Stuart was one such runner...

Chamonix, 1.5 Hours To Go

It's belting down and we all wonder how busy the start will be. I recall watching here last year in packed crowds and with the whole place jumping. But 11.30 at night in a deluge?

I do the essentials and hand in my drop bag for the half way checkpoint, then Annie makes an emergency call to a friend who lives in town: 'Joy, can we call in for a cup of tea, please?!' Thank God she's in, and we sit out the remaining wait time slowly steaming and dripping over her floor while checking the race updates online. Phil joins us half way through. He's got full media accreditation this year which means he's covering the entire race - someone else who will be pulling a two-night gig.

30 Minutes To Go

Back outside and the square is a sea of multicoloured waterproofs. People have appeared as if from nowhere, and if it's not in full jump mode, it's pretty close with the bedraggled MC's giving their all to whip up the crowd. I shout into Annie's ear 'I need to be over there!' A hug and kiss sends me on my way to squirm through the bodies to get as close as I can to the start gantry.

In the crowds, in the deluge at the race start Chamonix

I finally come to a halt about 50 yards away recalling that Stuart had said that would equate to around a five minute delay. If I turn my head I can see the big screen behind me which is showing shots of the front line of the start. There's Killian, Jez, Scott, Sebastian, Lizzy, all looking as reassuringly soaked as us mere mortals. All other movement is impossible so I try to relax and take it all in from under my hood. There's a lot to absorb: It maybe nearly midnight in godawful weather, but the square is packed, music is thumping, people hanging off balconies, and cameras going off everywhere. And even though I'm a repressed Englishman I can't help being drawn into the excitement...

Go!

A massive cheer, music cranked to maximum, a surge, then a stop, and we're off - kinda. It's stop start with bottlenecks frequent and a crowd who are going nuts. The emotion is almost overwhelming and to my astonishment I feel myself welling up as we shuffle between the barriers. I had absolutely not expected this but have some real wobbly lip moments and damp eyes as every so often a face in the crowd comes into focus and our eyes lock if just for a split second. What's conveyed in that connection? Excitement, joy, fear, awe and...love? All I know at the time is that it is enough to move me...

Clearing the town, I'm threading my way through the bodies as gaps open and trying desperately to avoid being skewered by a trekking pole. While around 50% of the elite field will use them, they are the kit choice of the majority as you go down the field. I have mine stashed and my plan is to use them from halfway. More bottlenecks as we enter the park. It's a large and clearly very scary puddle!

What the..?!?!

Ah, so continentals slow down for puddles, obviously.

I elbow through and splash down the middle leaving howls of derision in my wake.

Unbelievable.

The First Climb

It takes me around one hour of running along the valley bottom to find any meaningful space between the bodies - and I thought I'd got a reasonably good start position. An hour! I try very very hard to relax and just try to ease through as gaps appear but have to own up to the fact that impatience and claustrophobia get the better of me on more than a few occasions. Straight through the first checkpoint at 8km congratulating myself on avoiding any puncture wounds, and onto the approach to the first climb which will be a height gain of 800m in 6km to the high point at La Charme.

A sharp turn then boom! Straight up. This is our night run route with our clients, so not only is this whole next section familiar to me, it's familiar in the dark. I focus in on a relaxed and steady pace through the tarmac switchbacks which give way to muddy forest 4 x 4 trails. I seem to be steadily gaining ground without going into the red zone which is something to smile about as we thread our way upwards. And still people are out cheering on the course - not just a handful, but LOTS. Impromptu aid stations at the end of driveways, the noise of cowbells, entire families are out in the pouring rain at God knows what hour of the night.

We gain the top and I get ready for the 7km and 1000m plunge through the forest into St Gervais in the valley bottom. It's treacherous underfoot with much of the smaller paths now mud chutes. I bless my change of shoes and wonder briefly how many of the Europeans in their smoother shoes for the dry hardpacked trails will be getting on. I find that even being conservative and protecting my quads I'm passing folks here and there.

So it's a happy if very bedraggled chap who trots into the first big checkpoint at 21km to find once again the place is jumping and the soggy cameraman lining up on me is - 'Phil!'

"I love your work, Mr Mouncey"

"Wonderful to be working with you again, Mr Coates."

We indulge in a mutual grinning moment as I'm swift in and out gaining some more places in the process. I don't register it at the time but I'm already starting to pay for neglecting my eating and drinking in this first half marathon. One of the side effects in bad weather is that you just want to get your head down and get on with it - eating and drinking become less important, not least because the sensation of sweating is missing. And I've been remiss.

Into The Abyss

31km and we hit the checkpoint at Les Contamines after threading our way along and up and down the valley. I'm looking forward to meeting Annie and our runners for a boost before we hit the big desolate stuff.

Sure enough there's a smiling Annie with rice pudding and tea and an even more smiley welcome from Simon, Tiiu, Claudia and Lilly. I chow down and chat between mouthfuls realising that at last the rain has stopped but it's definitely colder here at 1100m. A handshake with Simon, kisses and soggy hugs from the girls and I head off on the approach to the longest climb and the high point of the race, the 1500m haul to the Croix de al Bonhomme at 45km some 2500m high.

As I leave the village I half register the time on a clocktower. I'd reckoned around 3.5 hours to this point - the leaders would have been through 30-40 minutes ago - and I'm sure I see clock hands at quarter past three.

There or thereabouts then...

My 21km face as captired by Phil Coates

But I'm now very cold and it takes me an age to warm up. I realise I'll have to stop and gear up before starting the long walk approach as the trail rises, and 4km later I do just that. On go the overtrousers, hat and gloves and out comes more food. Part of me registers the fact that I'm in France in August wearing full winter kit. Another part registers that it's been a very slow last 4km and that I'd better tune in 'cos there's a big-ass climb coming up.

So I walk, eat and do my best to appreciate the stars in a clearing sky. I'm on familiar ground having brought clients here over the last couple of years so know exactly what is coming. As we clear the forest and head ever higher, the landscape broadens out so that I can see a line of twinkling headtorches stretching out for miles ahead. I'm doing fine on the lower slopes but as the path steepens and I engage another gear my breathing suddenly spirals out of control and I'm having to fight to maintain my pace.

Bloody hell!

I'm both shocked and seriously uncomfortable and am forced to slow down to retain some semblance of control. Looking back on the steep switchbacks I can see I'm pulling what amounts to a train of about 20-30 people all following exactly the line I'm taking. To my amazement only a handful of these people charge past me on the steepest final part of the pull up to the col, but my attention is all over the place and suddenly I'm constructing all sorts of scenarios around packing it all in.

An abyss has opened in front of me and I'm heading straight down.

I realise the colour of the land is changing and am momentarily distracted from doing wallowing self-pity. It takes me a few seconds to make the connection: snow! Fresh snow on the ground which has also lightened the shape of the mountains around us as the wind now tries to blow us off the col. This is the point of no return. If I continue from here I'm committed all the way to the next valley floor checkpoint at 50km. And I can also turn back and retrace to Les Contamines and my own bed in our apartment. Fortunately I'm not thinking all that clearly and with most things on automatic I find my legs continue to carry me onward.

My mood is only momentarily lightened as I clock one of the Japanese runners who is clad only in a vest on his top half. Just a vest! Everyone else I can see has got full winter kit on here!

There's a final few km of rocky traverse and gentle climbing from the col to the refuge at the high point. I'd hoped to crack on from here, but am reduced to what feels like a shuffle. I have no energy for anything remotely upwards and my spirits have just spiralled.

Brighter, Briefly

As the world lightens around us I wander listlessly down to the refuge which marks the beginning of a 5km descent to Les Chapieux which will see us lose 1000m in height. The path is steep, frozen mud and shale going down and down as far as the eye can see. Treacherous in places. Above us is a different story: clear lightening skies start to highlight the mountains in a stunning early morning display showing off the new snowfall in all its glory.

But I'm still doing 'listless.'

Two thirds of the way down I start to pick up and by the time we hit the valley floor I've regained all the ground I lost on the climb - but I figure some serious calories are needed and proceed to make short work of two bowls of soup.

While I'm occupied I'm also chewing over the 'abyss' moment. I can see nothing good from that and a suspicion grows around some very empty reserve tanks. We'll know for sure on the next climb...

The next 40 minutes or so is the best weather window we'll get and we are treated to sunshine on the upper slopes of Mont Blanc ahead and to our left, clearing skies and freshly snow covered peaks. I've shucked my waterproofs, hat and gloves and rolled my sleeves up - a little precipitously because it's still very cold. I have to grab my hat and gloves back on before I've gone too far.

We're now on the 10km and 1000m climb to the Col de la Seigne and as the weather closes in once again around halfway up, my breathing spirals and I'm reduced to a slow walk. This time even my Japanese vest-wearing friend does nothing to lift my spirits. I'm moving too slowly to generate the heat I need to stay warm so despite full winter gear on again, I am also cold. Which just depresses me even further. I can see no possible way of breaking this pattern so I can see no possible way of completing this race. I reflect ruefully that, hey - at least the experiment's working and I'm getting some answers...

I am a truly sorry son of a b**** who shuffles over the frozen high point in what amounts to a near blizzard.

It's Just Not Working

We're now heading down to the Italian side of the Mont Blanc massif and the landscape changes accordingly. We are much closer to the towering walls and as a result it all seems much more dramatic as we emerge from the mist. I have moments when I am able to gawp in amazement at the scenery, but they are getting fewer as I do depression with more frequency.

We have one more climb to go before the long drop to Courmayeur and I realise I've decided: I will stop at Courmayeur. I also realise there is no lifting of spirits from that decision. I'm just too tired to care that much and anyway, there's still a way to go.

Despite all my mental skills I can still see no way to do another 50 miles and 5000m of climbing and descending once I reach Courmayeur. More importantly, I can't seem to make it matter enough either. I'm now paying the price for skimping the mental and emotional prep and figuring I could complete this little jaunt on what pretty much amounts to momentum. Lakeland was always my priority - this, (and the pre-race week) was an experiment. I was blasé and now it's back to bite me.

Full Stop

The fourth big climb is a 500 pull up to the Arrête du Mont Favre, a 2400m high point at 69km from which we start the 9km descent dropping 1200m into Courmayeur. The only way I can see me getting over this is with poles and so it proves despite my 'blow at halfway' pattern kicking in once again. I make time and places yet again on the descent as we drop into Italy and beautiful sunshine. I stop for an age at the final small checkpoint just faffing about before the steep drop through the forest into the town, preparing, I think, for it all to be over. The forest is quiet, beautiful, peaceful - and I am certainly calmer when I emerge.

It's taken me 78km & 4400m of climbing and descending to produce some answers to questions I probably had the answers to anyway - but sometimes the only way to really know is to do.

The inside showing on the outside. Showing the strain descending to Courmayeur

The Bigger Picture

The final race distance after the route changes was longer than normal: 107 miles

The finishing rate was 47%

35 hours into the race only 120 runners had finished.

Looking Back

I didn't think too deeply about this book to start with – just started going through my big race write-ups and realised that there was quite a collection over nearly ten years that maybe some folks would enjoy dipping in and out of.

Then Charlotte said: 'But we need something to link them all with, otherwise it's almost *so what?*' We racked our brains for ages till we came back to the only thing that they all had in common: me.

So I started to go back through my diaries. My earliest is actually a battered school jotter from 1983 – which makes me 17 – with a preamble noting that I'd actually started running 10 months earlier. The first entry on May 1st records details of my first half marathon in Ilkley, West Yorkshire:

Time 1 hour 30 minutes / Position 7th out of 60...weather appalling – absolutely pissing it down...race started half an hour late...realised afterwards I started off too slow 'cos I was fair burning down the last few miles...must perfect the drinking-on-the-run technique...on reflection the time was poor...reckon I can knock 15 minutes off it.

I was right, and I did – but it would take me another 8 years to do it.

What a window into my world that 1983 diary is. In that first year I'm running about 100 miles/month almost all of which are hard solo sessions on the same few courses against the watch – I remember diligently measuring the distances by string on a map - and even harder lunchtime sessions with my running school friends. I join my first running club Skyrac in the summer. Shin splints will strike in early 1984 but for now the progression is swift and it's obvious I seriously love the competition!

On Boxing Day of that year I – along with many other runners - line up for my local race without a number. The 7 mile Chevin Chase in Guiseley, West Yorkshire is still going today, but in 1983 rumours were rife that the then governing body of the sport, (the Amateur Athletics Association then going through its 'amateur versus professional' death throes) were out around the course noting numbers of club runners who dared to take part in this 'fun run'. I record that feelings were running high at the prospect of being listed as a 'banned runner.'

It was also a shock to re-discover that my ultra running career actually started 20 years earlier than I thought it had. In September 1983 my diary faithfully records how proud I was to be chosen to be part of our Venture Scout 'A' team to tackle the Six Dales Hike: Teams of 5 from the uniformed organisations link Settle and Swaledale in North Yorkshire via 42 linear off-road miles.

I remember full hiking kit being compulsory for the first three quarters, and how we were right at the forefront of footwear technology sporting the new radical (and first) lightweight leather boot from new company Walsh with its distinctive ripple sole. The organisers' only concessions to the search for a speedy traverse being that – bliss! - we were allowed to change into shorts and trainers for the last 10 miles.

I also recall that I was the upstart in our group and I remember the nerves as I worried about whether I'd be able to keep up with the big boys in our team. In the event, I was absolutely fine, it was someone else who dropped, and we placed 2nd in 8 hours 26 minutes. My diary records I was a wreck for a week, but clearly not that much as I still did a Sixth Form early hours nightclub party mid-week, (which always involved a curry and a 6 mile walk home) and a 4 mile road race the following weekend.

Young people, huh?

So, the more time I spent on the year-to-year links, the more I did the historical context bit, the deeper the book drew me in. I began to see patterns, trends, and have insights that had previously eluded me. Then other people who had seen a final draft got in on the act. What started as a series of separate race accounts has been revealed as a transformational journey covering the most significant period of my life so far.

I became a husband and a father – and I learnt to run for the thrill of the chase and the joy of each step.

In the days when national newspapers sponsored northern fellraces:
Penyghent, North Yorkshire 1984ish

Looking Forward

Yes, there is unfinished business at UTMB, but I wont be going back there this year. 2012 is about stepping away from the usual suspects. My year has revolved abound L100 for the last four, so when I do return to that start line I want to be hungry, excited and really ready.

The main fun and games will really start in the second half of this year as I start to build towards The Spine race on the Pennine Way in January 2013. Two hundred and seventy miles as continuously as possible will be the furthest I've travelled - and winter will no doubt up the ante somewhat. I will use a Bob Graham winter round in the English Lake District during December in the company of friends as a stepping stone.

My aspirations beyond that include the Barclay Marathons in the US - an outrageous event where the number of finishers since the first race in 1986 is still not much more than the fingers of both hands - and to bring ultra running into my *Transitions Changing Lives* programme.

As to the rest it is, as they say, all still very much a work in progress.

Other Publications

Soft back book London To Paris The Hard Way

In September 2003 Andy Mouncey became only the second person ever to successfully complete the Enduroman Arch to Arc Challenge. This solo triathlon comprises of an 87 mile run from London to Dover, swimming the 22 miles of the English Channel, then cycling 180 miles from Calais to Paris - all done as close together as possible. Andy set new fastest times for each of the stages. But Andy's journey was much more than simply running, swimming and cycling.This is his story.

"I just didn't move for 4 hours and read it from start to finish. Absolutely gripping."

"Finished it! I catch the train every day and this is my only spare time to read. I missed my stop TWICE!!"

"Finished the book which was a real roller coaster ride. This should be required reading for all endurance athletes and their other halves!"

This book tells the story of Andy's Arch To Arc odyssey from the early training swims to the triumphant last few metres in Paris. The story focuses on the Channel swim – the crux of the challenge – which is likely to be of greatest interest to the reader. Just how do you progress from the warmth and luxury of your local pool to taking on one of the toughest challenges in the swimming world?

But there is much more to Andy's narrative which also captures the raw emotions he experienced along the way in an entertaining style reminiscent of other books of this genre.

If you like big and scary, if you are harbouring desires to undertake your own big challenge, or you simply have sadistic tendencies then this is the book for you.

REVIEW BY TRIXTRA, BRITISH TRIATHLON ASSOCIATION WEBSITE

Buy the book

At www.bigandscaryrunning.com

or www.amazon.co.uk

Blog

Andy has an active blog at www.bigandscaryrunning.com where you can also find articles for download. He also writes periodically for running magazines.

Subscribe

Sign up at www.bigandscaryrunning.com to be kept up to date with Andy's latest posts.

Inspirational Speaking

Andy has been presenting to business, educational and sport audiences in this country and abroad since 2000.

Presentation 1: Doing Big and Scary

If you think this is another one of those 'look what I did, you can do it too' guys then think again. This really is unique, lively, entertaining... and it will really really move you."

Andy's keynote presentation about the essential insights from his Enduroman Arch to Arc Challenge: A 300 mile solo triathlon linking London and Paris - and swimming the English Channel is just the wet bit in the middle. Andy still holds the record for the fastest stages.

Brilliant! Spectacular! You gave us exactly what we wanted and the mix of humour, insight, and tips was spot on.

Adrian Batchelor St James's Place Wealth Management, London Area

Andy picks his audience up and transports them bodily onto the rollercoaster ride that was his own big scary journey. It is a powerful and moving mix of stories, humour, insight and audience interaction – and more: He will leave you in a very special place indeed.

Key Themes

- Competition Performance: Riding the mental & emotional rollercoster
- Make The Complex Simple: Big & scary goals by a six step process

- Personal Effectiveness: The authentic leader & role model
- Choosing Your Focus: Support & setbacks, persevering & learning
- Competition Performance with Managing Your Mood

It's so useful to have time for supported and focused reflection... I found some parts really moving.

CAROLE CRABTREE LUTON PRIMARY HEADS ASSOCIATION CONFERENCE

Presentation 2: Ultra Running Made Ultra Simple

Going 'long' and going 'off-road' is a trend that continues to pull in more and more runners looking for that next big challenge. Getting to the start line is the easy bit: Getting to the finish line requires a whole lot more.

In this powerful and inspirational presentation Andy uses his experience as an athlete and a coach to make ultra running appear ultra simple. Doing the training gets you to the start line. Andy will lift the lid on the three things that make the difference between a DNF and finishing with pride.

Ultra running is about being fit and durable, but more than that it is about your approach and attitude. The race tales and experiences Andy has pulled together provide an inspirational insight into how he has gone about achieving all that he has in the sport, becoming one of the most consistent performers around. There is a lot to learn. I hope you enjoy his stories like I did.

JEZ BRAGG, ULTRARUNNER AND UTMB WINNER 2010

Goals Setting Workshop

A 300 mile solo triathlon challenge linking London and Paris via an English Channel swim would teach you a thing or two about taking a big and scary next step.

A record-setting Enduroman Arch To Arc Challenge did just that for Andy Mouncey, and then he spent two years figuring out the 'how did that happen and so what anyway?' part.

He shares those key insights with you in this unique and powerful workshop and gives you a chance to practise with the key tools and techniques that were the foundation of his success.

Getting To Grips With Goals

"What a revelation after over twenty years of struggle!"
LEAD Business Leadership Programme, NW England

Andy cuts right to the heart of the matter so that you can make the goal-setting process simple, meaningful, effective and replicable.

He will put you in the right place ready to take your next big step.

Making It Real

"A colleague phoned me and said: 'Go see this guy speak – It's different, special and powerful.' So I did – and it is."
Steve Kempster Head of Business School, University of Cumbria

Andy's material is tried and tested in the big wide world. This means you get a workshop experience that is personal and memorable.

Take Home Tools

- A six part goal-setting template that you can take away and use.
- A process for adding emotion to a SMART goal so you can make it matter.
- A model of the 'flow' concept so you retain balance, get results and still enjoy your journey.

"It was simple, powerful, and easy enough for me to pass onto other people..."

LEAD BUSINESS LEADERSHIP PROGRAMME, NW ENGLAND

Coaching

Andy's range of coaching skills and experience has taken him into the corporate sector and into schools and colleges. In sport, he has worked with the English Institute of Sport and a range of athletes from weekend warriors to world class performers. Andy is currently the Run Course Director for trail running camps with Alpine Oasis.

Andy has the ability to engage athletes rather than simply instruct and discipline. This helps athletes to grow as people and take more responsibility for themselves and their actions.

DAVID TILLOTSON, REGIONAL MANAGER ENGLISH INSTITUTE OF SPORT

Residential Trail & Ultra Running Retreats in UK & France

Coaching and training for trail and ultrarunning in the UK and French Alps.

Andy is the resident coach for www.alpine-oasis.com and runs coaching days for ultra runners for www.gobeyondchallenge.co.uk

Triathlon For Schools

A modular programme for primary and secondary schools introducing pupils to the sport and using it as a basis for cross-curricular learning

Vibrant, engaging, provocative, thrilling. It brings stuff to life for the students and it stirs their emotions so that they turn them into actions. Realisation that achieving goals starts with the first step.

DR GRAEME MOORE DIRECTOR OF SPORT MILLFIELD SCHOOL

Transitions - The Transformational Change Programme

Transitions uses swim-bike-run as a means to engage marginalised young people and equip them with specific goal-setting and goal-achieving skills so that they can make a lasting transition back into mainstream education, employment and training, and a positive contribution to their communities

www.bigandscaryrunning.com

andy@doingbigandscary.com

tel: 07799 063 115